Those were the days ...™

Hot Rod & Stock Car Racing
in Britain in the 1980s

MOTAQUIP One word for parts

VELOCE

Other great books from Veloce –

Speedpro Series
4-cylinder Engine – How To Blueprint & Build A Short Block For High Performance (Hammill)
Alfa Romeo DOHC High-performance Manual (Kartalamakis)
Alfa Romeo V6 Engine High-performance Manual (Kartalamakis)
BMC 998cc A-series Engine – How To Power Tune (Hammill)
1275cc A-series High-performance Manual (Hammill)
Camshafts – How To Choose & Time Them For Maximum Power (Hammill)
Competition Car Datalogging Manual, The (Templeman)
Cylinder Heads – How To Build, Modify & Power Tune Updated & Revised Edition (Burgess & Gollan)
Distributor-type Ignition Systems – How To Build & Power Tune (Hammill)
Fast Road Car – How To Plan And Build Revised & Updated Colour New Edition (Stapleton)
Ford SOHC 'Pinto' & Sierra Cosworth DOHC Engines – How To Power Tune Updated & Enlarged Edition (Hammill)
Ford V8 – How To Power Tune Small Block Engines (Hammill)
Harley-Davidson Evolution Engines – How To Build & Power Tune (Hammill)
Holley Carburetors – How To Build & Power Tune Revised & Updated Edition (Hammill)
Jaguar XK Engines – How To Power Tune Revised & Updated Colour Edition (Hammill)
MG Midget & Austin-Healey Sprite – How To Power Tune Updated & Revised Edition (Stapleton)
MGB 4-cylinder Engine – How To Power Tune (Burgess)
MGB V8 Power – How To Give Your, Third Colour Edition (Williams)
MGB, MGC & MGB V8 – How To Improve (Williams)
Mini Engines – How To Power Tune On A Small Budget Colour Edition (Hammill)
Motorcycle-engined Racing Car – How To Build (Pashley)
Motorsport – Getting Started in (Collins)
Nitrous Oxide High-performance Manual, The (Langfield)
Rover V8 Engines – How To Power Tune (Hammill)
Sportscar/kitcar Suspension & Brakes – How To Build & Modify Enlarged & Updated 2nd Edition (Hammill)
SU Carburettor High-performance Manual (Hammill)
Supercar, How To Build (Thompson)
Suzuki 4x4 – How To Modify For Serious Off-road Action (Richardson)
Tiger Avon Sportscar – How To Build Your Own Updated & Revised 2nd Edition (Dudley)
TR2, 3 & TR4 – How To Improve (Williams)
TR5, 250 & TR6 – How To Improve (Williams)
TR7 & TR8 – How To Improve (Williams)
V8 Engine – How To Build A Short Block For High Performance (Hammill)
Volkswagen Beetle Suspension, Brakes & Chassis – How To Modify For High Performance (Hale)
Volkswagen Bus Suspension, Brakes & Chassis – How To Modify For High Performance (Hale)
Weber DCOE, & Dellorto DHLA Carburetors – How To Build & Power Tune 3rd Edition (Hammill)

Those Were The Days ... Series
Alpine Trials & Rallies 1910-1973 (Pfundner)
Austerity Motoring (Bobbitt)
Brighton National Speed Trials (Gardiner)
British Police Cars (Walker)
British Woodies (Peck)
Dune Buggy Phenomenon (Hale)
Dune Buggy Phenomenon Volume 2 (Hale)
Hot Rod & Stock Car Racing in Britain In The 1980s (Neil)
MG's Abingdon Factory (Moylan)
Motor Racing At Brands Hatch In The Seventies (Parker)
Motor Racing At Crystal Palace (Collins)
Motor Racing At Goodwood In The Sixties (Gardiner)
Motor Racing At Nassau In The 1950s & 1960s (O'Neil)
Motor Racing At Oulton Park In The 1960s (Mcfadyen)
Motor Racing At Oulton Park In The 1970s (Mcfadyen)
Three Wheelers (Bobbitt)

Enthusiast's Restoration Manual Series
Citroën 2CV, How To Restore (Porter)
Classic Car Bodywork, How To Restore (Thaddeus)
Classic Car Electrics (Thaddeus)
Classic Cars, How To Paint (Thaddeus)
Reliant Regal, How To Restore (Payne)
Triumph TR2/3/3A, How To Restore (Williams)
Triumph TR4/4A, How To Restore (Williams)
Triumph TR5/250 & 6, How To Restore (Williams)
Triumph TR7/8, How To Restore (Williams)
Volkswagen Beetle, How To Restore (Tyler)
VW Bay Window Bus (Paxton)
Yamaha FS1-E, How To Restore (Watts)

Essential Buyer's Guide Series
Alfa GT (Booker)
Alfa Romeo Spider Giulia (Booker & Talbott)
BMW GS (Henshaw)
BSA Bantam (Henshaw)
BSA Twins (Henshaw)
Citroën 2CV (Paxton)
Citroën ID & DS (Heilig)
Fiat 500 & 600 (Bobbitt)
Jaguar E-type 3.8 & 4.2-litre (Crespin)
Jaguar E-type V12 5.3-litre (Crespin)
Jaguar/Daimler XJ6, XJ12 & Sovereign (Crespin)
Jaguar XJ-S (Crespin)
MGB & MGB GT (Williams)
Mercedes-Benz 280SL-560DSL Roadsters (Bass)
Mercedes-Benz 'Pagoda' 230SL, 250SL & 280SL Roadsters & Coupés (Bass)
Morris Minor & 1000 (Newell)
Porsche 928 (Hemmings)
Rolls-Royce Silver Shadow & Bentley T-Series (Bobbitt)
Subaru Impreza (Hobbs)
Triumph Bonneville (Henshaw)
Triumph TR6 (Williams)
VW Beetle (Cservenka & Copping)
VW Bus (Cservenka & Copping)

Auto-Graphics Series
Fiat-based Abarths (Sparrow)
Jaguar MKI & II Saloons (Sparrow)
Lambretta Li Series Scooters (Sparrow)

Rally Giants Series
Audi Quattro (Robson)
Austin Healey 100-6 & 3000 (Robson)
Fiat 131 Abarth (Robson)
Ford Escort MkI (Robson)
Ford Escort RS Cosworth & World Rally Car (Robson)
Ford Escort RS1800 (Robson)
Lancia Stratos (Robson)
Peugeot 205 T16 (Robson)
Subaru Impreza (Robson)

General
1½-litre GP Racing 1961-1965 (Whitelock)
AC Two-litre Saloons & Buckland Sportscars (Archibald)
Alfa Romeo Giulia Coupé GT & GTA (Tipler)
Alfa Romeo Montreal – The Essential Companion (Taylor)
Alfa Tipo 33 (McDonough & Collins)
Alpine & Renault – The Development Of The Revolutionary Turbo F1 Car 1968 to 1979 (Smith)
Anatomy Of The Works Minis (Moylan)
Armstrong-Siddeley (Smith)
Autodrome (Collins & Ireland)
Automotive A-Z, Lane's Dictionary Of Automotive Terms (Lane)
Automotive Mascots (Kay & Springate)
Bahamas Speed Weeks, The (O'Neil)
Bentley Continental, Corniche And Azure (Bennett)
Bentley MkVI, Rolls-Royce Silver Wraith, Dawn & Cloud/Bentley R & S-Series (Nutland)
BMC Competitions Department Secrets (Turner, Chambers Browning)
BMW 5-Series (Cranswick)
BMW Z-Cars (Taylor)
Britains Farm Model Balers & Combines 1967 to 2007 (Pullen)
British 250cc Racing Motorcycles (Pereira)
British Cars, The Complete Catalogue Of, 1895-1975 (Culshaw & Horrobin)
BRM – A Mechanic's Tale (Salmon)
BRM V16 (Ludvigsen)
BSA Bantam Bible, The (Henshaw)
Bugatti Type 40 (Price)
Bugatti 46/50 Updated Edition (Price & Arbey)
Bugatti T44 & T49 (Price & Arbey)
Bugatti 57 2nd Edition (Price)
Caravans, The Illustrated History 1919-1959 (Jenkinson)
Caravans, The Illustrated History From 1960 (Jenkinson)
Carrera Panamericana, La (Tipler)
Chrysler 300 – America's Most Powerful Car 2nd Edition (Ackerson)
Chrysler PT Cruiser (Ackerson)
Citroën DS (Bobbitt)
Cliff Allison – From The Fells To Ferrari (Gauld)
Cobra – The Real Thing! (Legate)
Cortina – Ford's Bestseller (Robson)
Coventry Climax Racing Engines (Hammill)
Daimler SP250 New Edition (Long)
Datsun Fairlady Roadster To 280ZX – The Z-Car Story (Long)
Dino – The V6 Ferrari (Long)
Dodge Charger – Enduring Thunder (Ackerson)
Dodge Dynamite! (Grist)
Donington (Boddy)
Draw & Paint Cars – How To (Gardiner)
Drive On The Wild Side, A – 20 Extreme Driving Adventures From Around The World (Weaver)
Ducati 750 Bible, The (Falloon)
Ducati 860, 900 And Mille Bible, The (Falloon)
Dune Buggy, Building A – The Essential Manual (Shakespeare)
Dune Buggy Files (Hale)
Dune Buggy Handbook (Hale)
Edward Turner: The Man Behind The Motorcycles (Clew)
Fiat & Abarth 124 Spider & Coupé (Tipler)
Fiat & Abarth 500 & 600 2nd Edition (Bobbitt)
Fiats, Great Small (Ward)
Fine Art Of The Motorcycle Engine, The (Peirce)
Ford F100/F150 Pick-up 1948-1996 (Ackerson)
Ford F150 Pick-up 1997-2005 (Ackerson)
Ford GT – Then, And Now (Streather)
Ford GT40 (Legate)
Ford In Miniature (Olson)
Ford Model Y (Roberts)
Ford Thunderbird From 1954, The Book Of The (Long)
Forza Minardi! (Vigar)
Funky Mopeds (Skelton)
Gentleman Jack (Gauld)
GM In Miniature (Olson)
GT – The World's Best GT Cars 1953-73 (Dawson)
Hillclimbing & Sprinting – The Essential Manual (Short & Wilkinson)
Honda NSX (Long)
Jaguar, The Rise Of (Price)
Jaguar XJ-S (Long)
Jeep CJ (Ackerson)
Jeep Wrangler (Ackerson)
Karmann-Ghia Coupé & Convertible (Bobbitt)
Lamborghini Miura Bible, The (Sackey)
Lambretta Bible, The (Davies)
Lancia 037 (Collins)
Lancia Delta HF Integrale (Blaettel & Wagner)
Land Rover, The Half-ton Military (Cook)
Laverda Twins & Triples Bible 1968-1986 (Falloon)
Lea-Francis Story, The (Price)
Lexus Story, The (Long)
little book of smart, the (Jackson)
Lola – The Illustrated History (1957-1977) (Starkey)
Lola – All The Sports Racing & Single-seater Racing Cars 1978-1997 (Starkey)
Lola T70 – The Racing History & Individual Chassis Record 4th Edition (Starkey)
Lotus 49 (Oliver)
Marketingmobiles, The Wonderful Wacky World Of (Hale)
Mazda MX-5/Miata 1.6 Enthusiast's Workshop Manual (Grainger & Shoemark)
Mazda MX-5/Miata 1.8 Enthusiast's Workshop Manual (Grainger & Shoemark)
Mazda MX-5 Miata: The Book Of The World's Favourite Sportscar (Long)
Mazda MX-5 Miata Roadster (Long)
MGA (Price Williams)
MGB & MGB GT– Expert Guide (Auto-doc Series) (Williams)
MGB Electrical Systems (Astley)
Micro Caravans (Jenkinson)
Micro Trucks (Mort)
Microcars At Large! (Quellin)
Mini Cooper – The Real Thing! (Tipler)
Mitsubishi Lancer Evo, The Road Car & WRC Story (Long)
Montlhéry, The Story Of The Paris Autodrome (Boddy)
Morgan Maverick (Lawrence)
Morris Minor, 60 Years On The Road (Newell)
Moto Guzzi Sport & Le Mans Bible (Falloon)
Motor Movies – The Posters! (Veysey)
Motor Racing – Reflections Of A Lost Era (Carter)
Motorcycle Apprentice (Cakebread)
Motorcycle Road & Racing Chassis Designs (Noakes)
Motorhomes, The Illustrated History (Jenkinson)
Motorsport In colour, 1950s (Wainwright)
Nissan 300ZX & 350Z – The Z-Car Story (Long)
Off-Road Giants! – Heroes of 1960s Motorcycle Sport (Westlake)
Pass The Theory And Practical Driving Tests (Gibson & Hoole)
Peking To Paris 2007 (Young)
Plastic Toy Cars Of The 1950s & 1960s (Ralston)
Pontiac Firebird (Cranswick)
Porsche Boxster (Long)
Porsche 964, 993 & 996 Data Plate Code Breaker (Streather)
Porsche 356 (2nd Edition) (Long)
Porsche 911 Carrera – The Last Of The Evolution (Corlett)
Porsche 911R, RS & RSR, 4th Edition (Starkey)
Porsche 911 – The Definitive History 1963-1971 (Long)
Porsche 911 – The Definitive History 1971-1977 (Long)
Porsche 911 – The Definitive History 1977-1987 (Long)
Porsche 911 – The Definitive History 1987-1997 (Long)
Porsche 911 – The Definitive History 1997-2004 (Long)
Porsche 911SC 'Super Carrera' – The Essential Companion (Streather)
Porsche 914 & 914-6: The Definitive History Of The Road & Competition Cars (Long)
Porsche 924 (Long)
Porsche 944 (Long)
Porsche 993 'King Of Porsche' – The Essential Companion (Streather)
Porsche 996 'Supreme Porsche' – The Essential Companion (Streather)
Porsche Racing Cars – 1953 To 1975 (Long)
Porsche Racing Cars – 1976 On (Long)
Porsche – The Rally Story (Meredith)
Porsche: Three Generations Of Genius (Meredith)
RAC Rally Action! (Gardiner)
Rallye Sport Fords: The Inside Story (Moreton)
Redman, Jim – 6 Times World Motorcycle Champion: The Autobiography (Redman)
Rolls-Royce Silver Shadow/Bentley T Series Corniche & Camargue Revised & Enlarged Edition (Bobbitt)
Rolls-Royce Silver Spirit, Silver Spur & Bentley Mulsanne 2nd Edition (Bobbitt)
RX-7 – Mazda's Rotary Engine Sportscar (Updated & Revised New Edition) (Long)
Scooters & Microcars, The A-Z Of Popular (Dan)
Scooter Lifestyle (Grainger)
Singer Story: Cars, Commercial Vehicles, Bicycles & Motorcycles (Atkinson)
SM – Citroën's Maserati-engined Supercar (Long & Claverol)
Subaru Impreza: The Road Car And WRC Story (Long)
Taxi! The Story Of The 'London' Taxicab (Bobbitt)
Tinplate Toy Cars Of The 1950s & 1960s (Ralston)
Toyota Celica & Supra, The Book Of Toyota's Sports Coupés (Long)
Toyota MR2 Coupés & Spyders (Long)
Triumph Motorcycles & The Meriden Factory (Hancox)
Triumph Speed Twin & Thunderbird Bible (Woolridge)
Triumph Tiger Cub Bible (Estall)
Triumph Trophy Bible (Woolridge)
Triumph TR6 (Kimberley)
Unraced (Collins)
Velocette Motorcycles – MSS To Thruxton Updated & Revised (Burris)
Virgil Exner – Visioneer: The Official Biography Of Virgil M Exner Designer Extraordinaire (Grist)
Volkswagen Bus Book, The (Bobbitt)
Volkswagen Bus Or Van To Camper, How To Convert (Porter)
Volkswagens Of The World (Glen)
VW Beetle Cabriolet (Bobbitt)
VW Beetle – The Car Of The 20th Century (Copping)
VW Bus – 40 Years Of Splitties, Bays & Wedges (Copping)
VW Bus Book, The (Bobbitt)
VW Golf: Five Generations Of Fun (Copping & Cservenka)
VW – The Air-cooled Era (Copping)
VW T5 Camper Conversion Manual (Porter)
VW Campers (Copping)
Works Minis, The Last (Purves & Brenchley)
Works Rally Mechanic (Moylan)

www.veloce.co.uk

First published in July 2008 by Veloce Publishing Limited, 33 Trinity Street, Dorchester DT1 1TT, England. Fax 01305 268864/e-mail info@veloce.co.uk/web www.veloce.co.uk or www.velocebooks.com.
ISBN: 978-1-84584-167-6/UPC: 6-36847-04167-0

Readers with ideas for automotive books, or books on other transport or related hobby subjects, are invited to write to the editorial director of Veloce Publishing at the above address.
British Library Cataloguing in Publication Data - A catalogue record for this book is available from the British Library. Typesetting, design and page make-up all by Veloce Publishing Ltd on Apple Mac.
Printed in India by Replika Press.

Contents

Publisher's note. The photographs in this book were not ever intended for publication and are essentially an enthusiastic spectator's snapshots. We think that the real atmosphere the photos portray more than compensate for any lack of quality.

Acknowledgements & introduction

Acknowledgements

My very grateful thanks to the following for their help with this book ... Neil Clarke, Stuart Bradburn, Robert Edwards, Roger Fennings, Mark Haddleton & *Short Circuit* magazine, Sonny & Barbara Howard, Joerg Katstien, Steve McCall, Fergus McAnallen (Rally Retro), Graeme Mearns, David, Wendy, Jamie and Leah, Geert Roubroeks, Daniel Ruston, Spedeworth, Andy Weltch and all at Veloce. The book is dedicated to my wonderful wife Michele and my equally wonderful son Taylor.

Sources for research include the *Spedeworth Spedeweek* magazine, *Wheelspin* and *Short Circuit* magazine.

The role of honour in the appendix could not have been put together without the assistance of some of the sport's most ardent fans, who are included in the acknowledgements. In the text you will read references to races where the winners were disputed – these events were recorded by a lap scorer armed only with pen and paper, well before the advent of electronic timing with transponders. Sadly, the sport's record of keeping championship statistics is not much better either, and there may be the odd error or omission, for which I apologise. I hope, if you spot one, you will get in touch, and help us complete our archives.

Introduction

The 1970s left the sport of short oval racing in very good shape, with healthy domestic competition in all areas of the United Kingdom, plus the added bonus of promoters all beginning to co-operate much more on a regular basis to ensure that championships carried worthy titles.

Hot Rod racing led the way in this regard with its World Championship, an event that had not only attracted entrants from overseas, but also a fair representation of promoters and circuits from across the UK. This inter-promotional and inter-country cooperation meant that the formula was going from strength to strength, year on year throughout the 1970s. By the end of the decade the drivers were spending a lot of money on equipment and wanted to race together more than a couple of times a year – the usual key dates being the World and National Championships hosted respectively by Spedeworth (at Ipswich), and Hednesford Hills. In 1978, the National Hot Rod Promoters Association set up a Grand Prix Series which offered key meetings with promoters all around the country throughout the season. This allowed top drivers from the different organisations and regions to race each other regularly to establish just who was the UK's best Hot Rod racer.

Whilst the cream of the Hot Rods enjoyed the opportunity to race each other, there was no chance to establish who was the best in Formula Two Stock Cars. The class split into two during the early sixties and, despite one or two efforts at planned reconciliations, there were still two formulas racing – the BriSCA Formula Twos and Spedeworth's Superstox. Both were well supported and had some real superstars but they were never to meet up on circuit.

Formula One Stock Cars had also experienced a breakaway in 1975 when a group of disaffected southern drivers formed their own organisation to race on the Spedeworth and Promotasport circuits.

Richard John Neil

1980

The racing decade got under way with a test series out in South Africa, with a team of Spedeworth drivers comprising Super Rod racer Paul Conde, Stock Car drivers Eddie George and Eddy Aldous, Hot Rodder Paul Knight, and Superstox star Roy Eaton. To save the guys shipping their own cars to the series, the local promoter arranged for cars to be provided. However, as the preparation left something to be desired, sight-seeing trips had to be abandoned in favour of getting the cars organised. The series was a success and became something of a regular feature.

Back in the UK, the Hot Rods were racing in what was the third season of their Grand Prix, but the competition had a name change and was now to be known as the NHRPA Championship. Despite this change, most of the fans still stuck with the old GP title. Barry Lee had won the inaugural Grand Prix series in 1978, with Mick 'Duffy' Collard winning the following season. Duffy continued where he left off with a good start to the 1980 campaign.

The opening round was at Ipswich on Sunday 4th May with the grid being decided by ballot. The race was won by Collard from 13th on the grid with Lee second. Collard paid tribute to his mechanics who had worked through the night changing his engine after problems during the previous night's racing at Wimbledon. Although the 1980s were a long way from the 'racing every night' times of the early seventies, this does show how much the sport has changed since then, as these days there would never be a small domestic meeting hosted by the same promoter on the night before a big race!

The structure of the series was to differ in 1980

An early shot of West Country driver, Colin White, in action, racing his Vauxhall Chevette at the Lydden circuit round of the 1980 NHRPA Series. Also in view are PRI man, Mike Bennett (143), and 1980 World Champion, Mick Collard (19).

Ipswich 1980. Barry Lee's innovative 'skirted' Escort kicks up the dust as it heads back to his pit. Also in shot is Jim Mensley's Toyota (18).

from previous seasons. Rather than having all the drivers doing all the rounds, it was decided to open up the competition to a bigger field, with each driver doing fewer (selected) rounds. Things started to get messy when drivers began turning up to race in meetings in which they were not supposed to be scoring points ...

At the end of the series, Lee had regained his title, the official points table showing Nigel Murphy second with third a tie between Leon Smith and Paul Grimer.

The World Championship for Hot Rods saw a 'first'

in 1980 as the grid was to be decided by flying lap times rather than by ballot. The meeting was also one of the first to be filmed for release on video by Spedeworth, and, although the result looks particularly amateur, with the benefit of nearly thirty years' hindsight, at the time it was something of a breakthrough.

Mick Collard finally joined the other two members of Hot Rod racing's 'big three' to win the world title for the first time. Barry Lee was back racing in a drop snoot-bodied Escort for the first time since 1978, but his new

Ormond Christie in his Colt on his way to third place in the 1980 World Championship.

car was also adorned with skirts, supposedly to reduce air turbulence under the car – an idea borrowed from Formula One Grand Prix racing at the time. Lee finished second, at which point the tradition of English drivers dominating the results ended.

Ormond Christie had already made something of a name for himself in Hot Rods. His first car – a Ford Anglia raced in the mid-70s – had hardly set the world alight, but from there on the man and his machinery started to get results and attention. He'd won the British Championship in a Triumph Spitfire (after which sports cars were outlawed), then he had bagged some useful results in a Triumph Herald (also subsequently banned), and begun the 1980 season with a Colt that was good enough to take third place behind Collard and Lee. The strength of the Northern Ireland drivers was further underlined as Ivor Greenwood took fourth place in his more traditional Escort.

Ivor 'the Driver' Greenwood on the grand parade at Ipswich in 1980. The Belfast-based man is still involved in motor sport as a noted builder of racing engines.

Tyre smoke off the back of Nigel Murphy's Escort as he passes the 87 car of John Stone on the Turnstile bend at Ipswich. Ahead of them is Scottish ace, Kenny Ireland (196).

Spedeworth's first Banger Caravan race about to get under way with eventual winner, Graham Poulter (Jaguar 152), at the front of the field.

Kenny Cooke in the ex-works Opel Kadett at Wimbledon. The car was originally raced by Barry Lee for part of the 1979 season.

The support races included Spedeworth's first running of a Banger Caravan race, which proved a great spectacle, especially for the television cameras. The main drawback was the amount of clearing up to do afterwards. Brighton Basher, Graham Poulter (152), won the race.

In previous years the National Points charts used to run from January to December, but this system was deemed unfair to drivers qualifying for World Championships – in the case of the National Hot Rods it meant that a driver could effectively get into the top positions on the points chart by only racing from January to June – half a season. In order to ensure that only the top, committed drivers qualified for such events, the charts were restarted immediately after the formula's major championship. The first winner of the mid-year to mid-year Hot Rod Points Championship was Mick Collard.

The 1979 Hot Rod World Champion, Gordon Bland, upset a few people by retiring from the sport whilst holding the title; many felt that he should have completed the season as an ambassador for the sport. To add insult to injury he made his debut in BriSCA Formula One Stox in 1980.

East Anglian driver, Kenny Cooke, bought the ex-works, ex-Lee Opel Kadett and installed a Ford engine in it and made it go rather well. Popular Midlander,

Winner of the 1980 East Anglian Championship, Alan Dent, in his RS-bodied Escort at Ringwood.

A domestic line-up of PRI Hot Rods at Lydden circuit in Kent.

Superstox star, Howard Cole, about to take part in the grand parade at Ipswich. That's F2 ace, Bill Batten, driving the car. Batten, Cole and Ivor Greenwood were great friends, although they rarely raced together.

One of the top men in PRI Formula Three, Brian Holmes, at Arena Essex.

Blue-top Formula Three Stock Cars await the off at Arena Essex in 1981. Chris 'Charlie' Brown is in car 50, on his inside is Martyn Browne (8), and behind them is Vic Wiles (56).

Trevor Shaw, won two major titles: the British and the National at Hednesford in June and September respectively. Many fans rooted for drivers who raced on a limited budget, and there would have been some cheers at Ipswich on 22nd June when Alan Dent won the East Anglian Championship.

Spedeworth, which was never averse to inter-promotional cooperation, and fellow southeastern promoter, PRI, set up some team matches between their Superstox and F3 classes. The results were always going to be predictable wins for Spedeworth, as many of the PRI drivers were former Spedeworth men without

Mac McCarthy's immaculate 'Last Y' Superstox in the Aldershot pits.

the same budgets and with older cars than their rivals. Nonetheless, the inter-promotional cooperation was a welcome sight on the fixture lists. Brian Holmes was the first F3 driver to appear on a Spedeworth circuit when he guested at the open Champion of Champions event (won by Brian Stacey). The first team match was at Wimbledon on 19th April and the Spedeworth lads won 90-20. The return was at Arena Essex a week later with another convincing win (72-14) for the largely Ford-powered visitors.

Dave Pierce maintained his 1970s status of being the driver to beat in the Superstox, although the 1980s World Championship victory was only the second time

he had won the title – his first having been back in 1968! His dominance in the formula also saw him take the European title (held in Belgium), UK Challenge Cup, and Southern Championship. He was runner-up to Jim Welch (who retired at the end of the season) in the British. To recognise Pierce's incredible contribution to racing he was awarded a testimonial meeting at Aldershot on 29th October.

After the first ever staging at Ipswich in 1961, the Superstox World Championship found a home at London's Wimbledon Stadium from 1962 to 1974. Although the Hot Rods were, perhaps, a more cosmopolitan Formula, their own world title never moved from Ipswich. The premier Superstox race arguably became a more interesting affair as it ventured away from home for the first time in 1975, to Kaldenkirchen in Germany. East Anglian star, Neil Bee, won the race that year, with Scotsman, Gordon McDougall, winning on his home circuit, Cowdenbeath in 1976. The following year saw the race back at Wimbledon, with Jim Welch the surprise winner. This was a bit of a wake-up call for the Spedeworth drivers who, for the first time, had been beaten by a visiting (non-Spedeworth) driver – Welch was racing for Three Star Promotions at the time. McDougall took the title again in 1978, having impressively won away from home at Kaldenkirchen.

Winner of the 1980 Superstox Champion of Champions, Brian Stacey, pictured here on his way into the Wimbledon tunnel before a race.

The following year it was Welch again, this time at Great Yarmouth. The 1980 race was held at Cowdenbeath once again (on 17th August), and the smart money was on McDougall to take his third title – the Scots always having been difficult to beat on the unique Central Park circuit. In addition to the Scottish and English there was representation from Germany, Belgium, Holland and Northern Ireland. The English contingent was almost entirely from Spedeworth but Three Star Promotions sent its man, Mick Humphrey, hoping to emulate former colleague, Jim Welch's, feat three seasons back.

Unlike the Hot Rods, the Superstox stayed with the traditional public draw to determine grid positions, and it was local man, Ian Edmiston, on pole with future Spedeworth promoter Roy Eaton on his outside. It was a race of attrition, with Dave Pierce coming through from 16th on the grid to win the title. Although this was only the second time Pierce had become World Champion, he had held the mantle of National Points Champion for considerably longer than anyone else, and that was generally regarded as a much more difficult achievement.

A week later the PRI drivers contested their 'World' Championship at Crayford, although, with no overseas connections, or any other UK promoters represented, this was effectively a 'Club' Championship, the race being won by former kart racer, Simon Peters.

Sixties and seventies legend, George Polley, had not just returned to racing in Hot Rods, as, much earlier in the season, he had joined the Super Rods, racing Capri number 2: his first meeting was the Super Rods versus Rallycross team meeting at Wimbledon. Another returning name in the programme for that event was former Spedeworth Racing Manager, John Clark, who was competing in his Rallycross Porsche. John had been instrumental in several key areas of the short oval business, including establishing racing and contacts overseas, with, for example, some very successful links in South Africa. The Super Rods made good use of home advantage to win the match 102-73. Several of the Rallycross boys – including Clark – won races.

Polley, meanwhile, quickly became the man to beat in Super Rods, winning the 1980 European, National, English and East Anglian Championships. The National had taken place at Wimbledon with an interesting programme that included the British Championship for Minicross cars.

F1SCA cars were 'downsized' to a maximum engine capacity of 5 litres, in the hope of reducing costs and increasing driver numbers. The cars were to become known as F1SCA Formula 80, which was not a unanimously popular decision. With the demise of unlimited capacity F1SCA cars, and withdrawal of Spedeworth from Matchams Park, Ringwood, BriSCA ran a meeting for the 'original' group of BSCDA Formula One drivers at the Hampshire circuit. Formula 80 got under way at Wimbledon on 26th January with the grandly-named Open English Championship, which saw a heat and final win for Richard 'Sugar' Shergold, the other heat going to Les Mitchell.

Honours in the Bangers were shared around between Darwin Melboune (World Championship for the second successive year), Bill Bylett (National Figure of 8), and Mick Conlon (English). There were some notable team meetings as well – Spedeworth beating Norwich at Yarmouth by 89 points to 48, although the return match was closer (Spedeworth winning 55-50). Not so close was the trouncing of the south coast ARC team 105-0 at Aldershot!

Arguably the most important and revered team meeting took place at Wimbledon on 17th May, when Spedeworth played host to a team from PRI. This was the meeting of the two biggest players in the south of England, and the match lived up to all expectations: PRI won the first three races to lead 68-27, but suffered a great deal along the way. Spedeworth clawed its way back during race four, reducing the deficit to 78-50. To win the match the hosts had to shut out PRI from the top six. The visitors were not just shut out, they were totally demolished, with no finishers at all, which meant that Spedeworth ran out narrow winners, 80-78!

A return match at Arena was eagerly awaited though, sadly, abandoned due to misunderstandings over the match format. PRI would have to wait until the following season to see if it could avenge the defeat in the first ever match between the two teams.

George Polley was back racing both Hot Rods and Super Rods in 1980. This is the Capri he raced in the latter event.

1981

Spedeworth's circuit base was extended north to include the new tarmac track at Cleethorpes, and the first meeting there was on 28th June. Onchan Stadium on the Isle of Man, although not a Spedeworth circuit, hosted the Manx Motaquip Championship for Hot Rods, with 1980 World Champion, Mick Collard, winning on the rough circuit.

Spedeworth now decided to introduce another new formula. This time, however, it was not a lower budget version of an existing one, it was the Ministox class for teenage racers. At last, the southern short oval drivers had a class where their children could learn the ropes. As the name implies, the formula was an all-Mini affair, with the cars having ironwork similar to the Stock Saloons. The first Spedeworth race meeting for Ministox was held at Aldershot on Saturday 29th March 1981, with Super Rods and Bangers also on the bill. The races were won by Paul Warwick (of whom we'll hear more later) and Steve Girling. The other drivers making history that night by completing the line-up were; Mick Widgery, Paul Newman, Mark Barham, Andy Gosden, Dougie George, Tracy Stevens, Mark Butler, and Terry Hall.

When the Ministox had a published points chart for the first time, it was Mark Barham who had the honour of being the first silver-top in the formula.

Former Superstox World Champion, Gordon McDougall, started his own promotion at the Newtongrange circuit, after falling out with Spedeworth Scotland's Roy Cecil. This caused a split in the ranks in all the formulae north of the border, as drivers defected from Spedeworth's Superstox to McDougall's GMP promotion, which was running BriSCA Formula Two. GMP's class was always going to be the stronger of the two, as many English drivers were willing and able to commute to Scotland to race.

Despite the apparent attempts at inter-promotional cooperation, elsewhere there were still some ridiculous anomalies in the sport. One of the most glaring examples was multiple F2 Stock Car Champion, Bill Batten, who was also racing Hot Rods. He could compete in F2 at Newtongrange – and indeed he won the Scottish Championship there – but the Hot Rods at Newtongrange were not part of the National Promoters' Association. He could, of course, race the Hot Rod thirty miles away at Cowdenbeath, but at *that* venue he would have been banned by BriSCA for racing his F2 with the Superstox!

The Spedeworth Scots still managed to send two decent drivers to the World Superstox Championship, which headed back to Kaldenkirchen in Germany. Now being held on mainland Europe, the field was certainly graced with more top Europeans than usual, but neither Three Star nor PRI found themselves with any representation on the grid. Neil Bee drove from his mid-grid draw to win his second world crown from Dave Pierce and Paul Pearson, and a notable place man was Northern Ireland's lone representative, Jimmy Greenwood, who took fourth.

The other Championship results show that the racing was as competitive as ever. Brian Randall had his best-ever season, winning both the National and English Superstox titles, whilst Bill Bridges had his best result in the formula, as well as bagging the British at Wimbledon in September. Dave Willis won the season-opening Winternational, and Dave Pierce was European Champion, as well as runner-up in four other big title races, therefore claiming the national Points Championship once again.

After a long wait, the Spedeworth versus PRI Banger Team Races resumed at Arena on 21 June. Thirty two

Superstox legend Dave Pierce heading out to the track at Arlington in 1981. Behind Pierce is Dave Willis, and the youngster in the red overalls to the right of shot is Willis junior, Mark.

cars from each promoter fought it out over two heats, and, in the final, PRI did a grand job of seeing-off the opposition; there were no Spedeworth finishers in the last race, and PRI took the win 85-25! The return match was held at Wimbledon two weeks later, with the 'racing' again resembling a series of demolition derbys. The result was so close that a re-count had to take place, after which the Spedeworth team was deemed the winner by a single point (56-55).

"It had to happen sometime," was the phrase

Kent driver, John Stone, surprised race fans by taking over at the top of the National Points Chart in 1981.

laps before Christie came through, but the pair were to remain in combat until the champion retired. Evans then closed in on Christie and tried a last corner move, but it was Christie who took the title in his Toyota Starlet from Evans in the Chevette. The face of Hot Rod racing was set to change!

The Hot Rod season was fiercely competitive – Pete Stevens won the National, Barry Lee won the British, and Stu Jackson claimed the English title, and the Spedeworth silver roof was taken out of the hands of the usual suspects, when Kent racer, John Stone, topped the chart in August.

Many thought the Irish drivers were quick in the World Championship because of the similarity in size between Ipswich and their home tracks. Christie, however, was good wherever he raced, and he backed up this theory by winning the European title at the tiny, tricky Newton Abbot circuit in Devon just a fortnight after claiming the gold roof.

The NHRPA Championship became a single meeting rather than a series of championship rounds – so the best of the country's drivers assembled at Ipswich in November. Former English Champion, Colin Facey, won the race from Scotsman, Malcolm Chesher, Midlander, Peter Grimer, and South Westerner, Ken Salter.

echoing around Foxhall Heath, when the Motaquip World Hot Rod Championship was won by a non-Englishman for the first time. (In actual fact, there is a school of thought that believes that a South African, Bobby Scott, won the Championship back in 1972, rather than the officially-announced winner Bob Howe, but that is a matter for debate elsewhere. The South African representative this particular year, however, Anton Alberts, was officially slowest in qualifying.) At the sharp end it was defending champ, Mick Collard, who secured pole from the Northern Ireland pairing of Ormond Christie and Davy Evans. Collard led for 14

Autospeed driver, Martin Farrell, was one of the few to race an Avenger in the Hot Rods. He took part in the NHRPA Championship at Ipswich, late on in the season.

Dave Rackham was tipped by many to become one of the country's top Hot Rod drivers. Sadly, he was not racing long enough to realise his potential, although he made a good impression on the formula with a well turned-out car.

Two East Anglian drivers were prominent in the Stock Car title listing. Dick Doddington won the English and London events, whilst Graham Overy came first in the British and East Anglian races. Mr Consistency over the whole season, however, was Wally Hall who won the national points title.

Another Super Rod versus Rallycross encounter was held at Wimbledon, and the host formula won again 220-170. Looking back, these team matches were close enough to be entertaining, but showed how much more variety

One of the more unusual Stock Saloons from the 1981 season – the Opel Manta of Sussex star driver Brian Sayers.

Steve Dance was a multi-champion in Super Rods, who later became a successful Hot Rod and long circuit racer.

there was in the cars being used by the Rallycross team – Porsches, Minis and Escorts – against the virtual Ford Capri-monopoly of the Super Rods.

Back in the early 1970s, Spedeworth had run some end-of-season races with a mixture of formulae, called Spede Prix. This could well have been the inspiration for

Gordon Bland retired from Hot Rods at the end of his World Championship-winning season. He then went briefly into Formula One Stox before joining the Super Rods with this smart Capri.

the Champion of Champions race, which was contested by Super Rods and Hot Rods. Ten cars from each formula started the race, and it was British Super Rod Champion, Dick Hillard, who won from pole position, with Steve Crewe (Hot Rod) and Alan Dent (Hot Rod) in second and third places.

Gordon Bland re-appeared on the non-contact racing scene in the Super Rods, and netted the biggest individual title, the European Championship. Steve Dance won the Spedeworth points championship.

1982

The year got under way with the now-annual Winternational meeting, at Wimbledon. This event had its roots back in the mid-seventies, and had experienced some memorable meetings, such as the Hot Rod versus Rallycross team event, at the end of 1975.

Like the World Championships held every summer at Ipswich, this meeting was now televised live by ITV on *World of Sport*. Barry Lee, fully recovered from broken ribs sustained in practice for the previous season's National Championship, broke new ground for coverage of the sport, by running with an on-board camera. The equipment proved so bulky that it completely hampered his efforts, and the shale splattering onto the lens did

little for the picture either! Ormond Christie was taking his duties as World Champion very seriously, not only did he attend the event, but took a good win as well – all the more remarkable when you consider he was not used to racing regularly on shale.

Another South African tour took place over the winter months, with Christie again proving to be a worthy ambassador for the sport, this time joined by English drivers Steve Crew, John Stone and the Grimer Brothers. An unusual date which stood out in the early season fixture list was a Stock Rod 'chicane race' at Aldershot on 6th March – part of the Southern Championship meeting.

The increasing profile of racing in Northern Ireland was demonstrated, as the Hot Rod Supporters' Club organised a two day motor show at the Antrim Forum. Other classes were included too, such as the Super Rods, which were being introduced to Ulster that year. The Ulster Hot Rod drivers were rapidly making the move to Japanese machinery, with several drivers following Ormond Christie's Toyota Starlet example, although only one, raced by former Irish Open Champion, 'Sticky' Torrens, used a Toyota engine to power it. Other Nippon models coming to prominence

The Metro never quite captured the imagination of drivers or spectators in the way the original Mini did. The first of a few built and raced in Hot Rods was Micky Elliott's smart example.

Left: The Grimer brothers, Paul (8) and Peter (88), on a visit to Wimbledon stadium for the 1982 Winternationals. Also in frame are Paul Farnish (41) and Dicky Butler (63).

were the Toyota 1000, raced by Norman Woolsey, and the Mazda 323, raced by John Murray.

Whilst most of the top Irish drivers were busy going 'hybrid,' George Polley made the decision to go back to racing a Ford Anglia. Ironically, his Escort had just started to run well. George was high up in the points chart, and so had no worries about qualifying for the world final. Those that did, at least had the opportunity to qualify via a semi final for the first time. Peter Grimer won the semi from fellow, last-gasp qualifiers, Pete Winstone and John Carding.

The World Championship results were not

Davy Evans' World Championship-winning, Ford-powered Vauxhall Chevette.

suprising, as the gold roof and the trophy went back to Northern Ireland. This time, however, it was the popular Davy Evans who took the honours, with Hednesford's Stu Jackson in second, from his Midlands colleague, Peter Grimer. This was the first Hot Rod World Championship that had not seen a Spedeworth driver in the top three – the highest-placed 'home' driver was John Stone, in fourth position, in his first appearance in the race.

The most prolific winner in the major Hot Rod Championships was Pete Stevens, who scooped both the European and National Championships, at Ballymena and Hednesford respectively. Peter Grimer showed his liking for Ipswich, winning the NHRPA meeting there in November.

At the end of 1981, several PRI drivers had approached the promotion about running Stock Saloons for category, for the first time. The regulations for the class were similar to the Spedeworth formula, although,

The Ford Capri was one of the first cars of choice for the PRI Stock Saloon brigade. This fine example, piloted by star driver, Ron Coventry, has clearly been at the sharp end of the action.

with a typical lack of cooperation, the upper engine-capacity limits were different – with PRI set at 3.3-litres, as opposed to Spedeworth's which stood at 2.7. The first race for the class was on the big, Lydden oval in Kent, with Steve Pascoe winning in his 3-litre Ford Capri.

The Superstox World Championship continued its nomadic search for a new home, and was held at Cleethorpes Garden Stadium for the first time. Two years after the Hot Rods had adopted the system for their own World final, the Supers also had time trials, rather than a ballot, to determine the grid positions. There was also another similarity with the Hot Rods, a driver from Northern Ireland was to make his mark – in qualifying at least – as Ian McKnight set the fastest time, with his F2 specification 1.300cc car. (1.3-litre?) Defending champion, Dave Pierce, was starting alongside, with John Gray on row two, next to Neil Bee. As usual for

the Superstox, the grid was fairly cosmopolitan, with English and Northern Irish drivers being joined, as ever, by the Scots, along with three Germans and a Dutchman. Inter-promotional cooperation was also evident, as former Spedeworth man, Phil May, took to the grid along with Derek Pullman, the pair representing PRI. McKnight lasted no more than a lap and Pierce had mechanical problems, however, this should take nothing away from Neil Bee, who reclaimed the title for the first time since his 1970s win at Kaldkirchen in Germany.

The nature of the politics within the sport became evident, when two PRI drivers took part in the BriSCA Formula Two World Championship, at Smeatharpe. All short oval fans the length and breadth of the country would have loved to have seen a showdown between the likes of Superstox stars, such as Dave Pierce and Neil Bee, and Formula Two heroes, like Bill Bartten (who won the 1982 championship) and Malc Locke, but the politics would not allow it. They would, however, allow PRI to be represented at both events. The PRI representatives in the BriSCA version were Kiki Englezou and Jimmy Bryan, who were flying the flag for Cyprus and Jamaica respectively.

Pierce might have been out of luck at Cleethorpes, but he was in stunning form in the European Championship at Cowdenbeath, won in near-monsoon conditions. This race had seen the traditional draw for grid positions, with both Pierce and Bee on row two. It was far from easy for them from there, but Pierce

Spedeworth produced a special souvenir programme for its 1982 Masters Series.

Multiple Superstox champion, Steve Monk, pictured at Arlington in 1982.

managed to lap everybody, up to and including the third-placed Les Clark. This was the fourth European Championship win in a row for Pierce, and took him one ahead of Tony May in the record books, who had

won in 1967, 68 and 72. Another notable championship win was for Dave Willis, who won the British Superstox Championship at Wimbledon.

A 'one-off' for the formula was the £1000 Masters Series, which was contested in ten rounds at all of the Spedeworth tracks. It was unusual in that all the cars ran on Avon racing tyres, rather than the less-expensive and harder-wearing rubber they were used to, and this had a couple of implications. Quicker lap times were possible, and the change in handling almost always required changes in suspension set-up. The whole concept was perhaps seen as a toe-in-the-water exercise, as many felt that if the cars ran successfully on the racing tyres, it may be professional to continue their use. The line-up was by invitation, to fifteen of the top drivers at the time: Roy Eaton, Howard Cole, Dave Turner, Steve Monk,

Roy Eaton was top points scorer, and the grand final winner, of the Superstox Masters Series.

Dave Willis, Martyn Brand, Bill Bridges, Brian Randall, Neil Bee, Brian Jones, Robin Randall, Dave Pierce, Paul Pearson, John Gray and Derek Hales. Each round had two reverse grid races, (with clutch starts as opposed to the normal rolling starts), with the points from each round being amassed to determine the grid positions for the final, which took place at Wimbledon in October.

1974 World Champion, Steve Monk, dropped out of the series before it got under way, for budgetary reasons, and his place was taken by Jim Davey. The top points scorer over the year was Roy Eaton, and he duly converted his pole position at the Wimbledon final into a race win, ahead of Dave Turner and John Gray. Opinion differed amongst the drivers as to whether racing tyres *were* the way forward; the majority, however, was not

in favour of such a drastic change, and the exercise was never repeated.

One of the more unusual designs of Superstox to emerge came from Nottingham-based driver, Barry Watson, whose new car was actually based on a spaceframe chassis and left hand drive, rather than the central seating position of the traditional Superstox. The body was a nice, cut-down Marina, which extended across the width of the car.

The 1982 season was remarkable for the first running of the Stock Saloon World Championship, held at Kaldennirchen in Germany, and it was something of a surprise when home driver, Ditlev Katstien, came home as champion.

The Grand Prix Midgets had an away day, racing

Believe it or not – a Superstox. Barry Watson's fine spaceframe Marina-bodied car.

in Scotland for the first time on 8th August. Eleven cars made the trip and put on three entertaining races. 1977 World Champion, Mick Bonner, was quickest to adapt to the Central Park circuit, winning a heat and the final. The other race was won by the multiple champion, Malcolm Goodman. During the season, Gordon McDougal's promotion added Armadale to its ranks, but 1992 was a sad year for Spedeworth Scotland, as the man who had started it all up north o' the border, Roy Cecil, passed away.

At the end of season, on 27th November, Spedeworth ran a 'mixed car and motocross bike' meeting at Aldershot. John Steward, (480 Honda – not believed to be a relation to the noted car racer), won all three races. Mick Dean (250 Honda), was second in the final, from Trevor Pope (490 Maico). A similar fixture was held again at Aldershot, before the 1983 season got under way.

The top three drivers in the first World Stock Saloon Championship, held at Kaldenkirchen, Germany. Left to right; Keith Jarman (2nd), Detlev Katstein (winner), Hans Frey (3rd).

1983

Eight of the top Hot Rod drivers from Northern Ireland made their first trip to Tipperary, in the south. Some of the Tipperary drivers had already bought, and were racing, current, top specification cars, and this was to be the start of a healthy relationship with the circuit.

The first major event of the year for the Hot Rods was the English Championship at Wisbech stadium, in May.

Peter Grimer bagged it, his third major career title, as he'd won the English back in 1978 at Buxton, and, of course, the previous year's NHRPA. Kenny Cooke had put Barry Lee's old Opel Kadett on pole, with George Polley qualifying in second. Polley, however, had to retire from the race with a puncture, which left Cooke comfortably in front, until he tangled with back-marking Derek Hales. Grimer, therefore, took over at the front. Kenny Cooke, in probably one the best races of his career, then came back past several top drivers, including Barry Lee, to take second.

Grid line-up for the start of the 1983 World Hot Rod Championship. Ormond Christie has pole position, with Andrew Dance sharing the front row. Behind them is defending champion, Davy Evans, with Stu Jackson, Chris Griggs, and Peter Grimer.

Typically close Hot Rod action, with Barry Lee taking an outside line on another multiple champion, Pete Stevens.

Ormond Christie regained the World title at Ipswich, but that was the only major he got his hands on in 1983. The ever-consistent and quick Pete Stevens had a decent season, winning the European Championship in Belgium, and the National, again, at its traditional home of Hednesford. Mick Collard won the British at Newton Abbot, and Ulsterman, Leslie Dallas, was finally victorious, when he secured the end-of-season NHRPA at Ipswich.

The Superstox finally switched to the 2-litre Ford Pinto engine in an attempt to cut costs, although the move was made compulsory mid-season, rather than at the beginning of a new one. Generally, this change was felt to be good for the formula, and several drivers returned to the class. Some, who hung onto their more expensive Ford race engines, switched to Hot Rods. The drivers in Scotland, and on mainland Europe, were still using Ford short-stroke racing engines however, and this helped rapid Dutchman, Antony van den Oetelaar, to become the first non-UK driver to win the crown, the race taking place at

Mick Collard had two cars at the 1983 Spedeweekend, but his new Mazda was the choice for the grand parade. Barry Lee is the passenger.

Double World Superstox champion, Antony van den Oetelaar, gets crossed up at Ipswich.

The Mick Collard Escort leads the Mick Collard Mazda in practice!

Cleethorpes for the second year in a row. His countryman, Jo van Rengs, was second, with Scotsman, Les Clark, in third. England's chances in international races were further dented when Neil Bee was suspended from racing for twelve

A reasonably cosmopolitan group of Superstox. Robin Randall is heading out of shot, with Dutchman, Wiel Hermkens (10), Phil May (183), and Scotsman Bill Pullar (81) behind him.

John Coupland leads the way in the Super Rods, from Barry Goddard, Dick Hillard (31), Richard Chilton (07), and Mick Robertson (52).

months, just before the World final, over an engine irregularity.

The best drivers soon got to grips with the Pinto though, and were still notching up good results, whilst new drivers were increasing in numbers on the grids. Top Englishman in the championship stakes was, once again, Dave Pierce, who won the European Championship for the fifth time in succession – a record which still stands today.

The Superstox English Championship had a habit of producing suprise winners, and this year proved to be no exception, as Wimbledon specialist, Jim Davey, took his first and only major title win. Another 'new' name also appeared on one of the majors, as Tony Roots won the

Stock Saloons kick up the dust during the 1983 National Championship race. Ray Goudy (156) heads this pack, with Jayne Bean (37), Ian Sutton (101), Geoff Morris (591), and Robert George (229) also prominent in shot.

Superstox National Championship, at the Ipswich Spedeweekend.

The Super Rods continued to attract some quality names who wanted affordable racing, and this was evident as former Midlands Hot Rod star, Jon Brookes, won the British and English Championships in the formula. Former European Hot Rod Champion, Pete Winstone, came away as Points Champion, but unusually did not manage to win any of the big, single race titles.

In the Stock Cars, the English Spedeworth drivers were again denied the World title, as Gordon Brown won on home tarmac, north o' the border at Cowdenbeath. The European Championship was held at Kaldenkirchen, in Germany, with another home driver, Bert Houben, taking the title.

Stock Rods were increasing in number, and competition was becoming stronger at a national

Stock saloon stars, Keith Jarman and Harry Burgoyne, acknowledge the usual enthusiastic support of the Scottish fans, at Ipswich.

Two brutal Formula 80 cars in action at Ipswich. Pete Jones chases Paul Diamond.

level, despite the fact that the formula still had something of a stigma attached to it, as one of the cars 'to have' was the Austin 1300. The premier race in the category was the European Championship, held at Cleethorpes, which was won by Scotsman, Ian Bell, (who also won the British title) from Dave Braggins in second, and Brian Smith in third. Braggins went on to be a noted Mini racer on the big circuits, whilst Smith was to be around in Stock Rods for the best part of another 20 seasons.

Spedeworth began a short tenure at the small, shale circuit at Mildenhall. Oddly, the opening date was after the end of the regular season, on 20th November. The first race under the Spedeworth banner was for Superstox, and was won by white top driver, Zeph Eastell.

Stu Blyth's immaculate Formula 80 car, in the Paddock at Ipswich. Stu won the 1983 British Championship for the class at Cleethorpes.

1984

No new formulae arrived in 1984, although there was a change of name, as F1SCA Formula 80 Stock Cars became known as Spedeworth Formula One. The class was still not intended as competition for the national (apart from the south east!) BriSCA F1 Stock Cars, but as a more cost-effective alternative for the Spedeworth-licensed Southern drivers. The specification for the Spedeworth version remained at 5-litres. One of the best at driving and preparation in this class, Stu Blyth,

Top circuit racer, Dave Coyne, enjoyed a few outings in the Norman Abbot Rent-a-Rod. This shot captures some trademark Hot Rod opposite lock, as he dices with 1986 Winternational winner, Andy Grout.

Impressive line-up of Hot Rods at the 1984 Winternationals at Wimbledon. The back row (nearest camera) has Leslie Dallas and Mick Collard, with Spedeworth Racing Manager, Ray Wood, in attendance, just to the right of Collard's Toyota Starlet.

Stock Saloon driver, Eddie George, races around Wimbledon, despite having a fire in the car. The regular infield markers have disappeared – the cars are actually using the speedway bend. Scotsmen, Keith Jarman and Bob Jones, are on the inside line.

kicked off the year in good style at Wimbledon, by winning the English Championship.

Many promoters were still running their own variations of classes, up and down the country, but it was heartening to see that more and more were coming into line, to create a truly National formula that could compete together in major races. The class that benefited most from this, in the 1984 season, was the Ministox, as it was introduced by both Spedeworth Scotland and Hednesford. The latter's first meeting was an invitation, and saw the first race win going to Steven Carding, son of Hot Rod racer, John.

In 1983, the PRI Hot Rods had contested a one-off meeting, on the Indy Circuit at Brands Hatch. The layout, not quite an oval, with two left hand corners at Graham Hill Bend and Surtees, proved well suited to the class, and the reversed grid racing had proved popular

Sean Brown was one of several short oval drivers who moved into circuit racing. Hot Rods had evolved sufficiently to enable the cars to be competitive on the long tracks. Although Sean could have taken part in the Hot Rod races at Brands in 1984, he is pictured here participating in a modified saloon event.

PRI Hot Rodder, Les Giddy, enjoying the open space, in one of two meetings held for the formula at Brands Hatch.

with the organisers; so, two more dates were added for the formula, in April and August 1984. The crossover between short ovals and long circuits was happening elsewhere, as Hednesford planned a meeting that would include short oval racing for the single-seater racing category, Formula Ford 1600. Although the meeting did not happen, a similar idea was put into practice in Europe a few seasons later, using Formula Toyota cars.

At this time, however, the English Midgets were doing well. It had become a self-governing club back in 1975, and found its own fixtures with promoters. One of the dates in 1984 was the World Championship, at Northampton. This was another meeting shown live on ITV's *World of Sport*, and the truly international nature of the event certainly did the class no harm. The race itself was exciting too, with Alf Boarer, driving from the back of the grid, to take the lead from Mick Bonner on the last bend, winning the title.

PRI realised that getting more than one use out of a stadium was good for business, and so Speedway was introduced to Arena Essex on 5th April – the shale track being laid on the inside of the tarmac oval used for car racing. The Essex Hammers were to become an established part of the UK Speedway scene.

One of the top names from the UK Hot Rod racing scene looked like he would be on his way out of the formula, after some winter outings in Rallycross. 1982 World Champion, Davy Evans, was citing frustration with Hot Rod racing at the time, but in all probability he may have felt he was not reaching his full potential, racing on the short ovals. Rallycross outings at the Boyd Autodrome, and at Mondello Park, got him seriously thinking about moving into rallying, and he made his debut in the sport in the Circuit of Ireland Rally, co-driven by Roy Kernaghan. In his first competition against such highly regarded names as Jimmy McRae and Henri Toivonen, the result was an amazing third place. His impressive introduction to the sport continued in major events, and later in 1984

Top man in the Grand Prix Midgets during 1984 was Alf Boarer. Alf is pictured at speed in his smart BMC-powered Arrow car.

Davy Evans in action in his first big rally – the 1984 Circuit of Ireland. Evans stunned the rally world with third place in his Nissan 240RS.

he scored a 6th place in the Manx International Rally, and a 4th place at the Cork International Rally, finishing 3rd in points in the 1984 Irish Tarmac Series.

Superstox were in for a good year, as Paul Warwick graduated to the formula from Ministox. He first raced his Colin Higman chassis at his home circuit, Aldershot, in a wet meeting at the end of March, although a final win would elude him until almost a month later, after taking several heats, when he won the feature, again at Aldershot. Everyone knew that Paul would shine in the class, but his rapid progress still managed to raise an eyebrow or two, especially when he became the youngest driver to win the National Championship, at just 16 years of age, at the Ipswich Spedeweekend.

Warwick's arrival may have been good for the Superstox, but, as one hero arrived at the beginning of the year, another departed the scene at the end, with Dave Pierce's retirement from the formula. The Dorking man raced for the last time at Aldershot, on Boxing Day 1984, leaving a legacy of championship wins from what

Davy Evans being interviewed in front of City Hall, Belfast, on the finish ramp after the Circuit of Ireland.

Young Superstox superstar, Paul Warwick, in action during his second and final season of racing in the formula.

Things are getting a bit hectic in the Superstox, as Howard Cole (211), finds himself broadside across the bend, right in front of Gerry Cooper (the yellow car with the red roof).

was undoubtedly the sport's most competitive era.

Although there was a trend in Hot Rods at this time to move towards more 'hybrid' cars, many of the formula's new drivers were doing well with more traditional machinery and modest budgets. One example was former Stock Saloon and Banger racer, Martin Davey, who had done well with a Ford Anglia.

The final few entries to the Hot

A touch of understeer for Mark Eaton in the Superstox.

Another win for Dave Pierce – one of the all-time greats in Superstox, who retired from the sport on Boxing Day, 1984.

Rod World Championship were to be decided by semi finals again. One of these, down at Newton Abbot in Devon, provided a controversial ending, as John Edwards apparently took Stu Jackson into the wall, allowing Leon Smith through to win from two local stars, Spence Morgan and Derek Palmer.

The World title finally returned home to England, with Peter Grimer steering his Ford-powered Toyota Starlet to both pole position and the race win. George Polley was second, his best result in the event since winning the crown back in 1976, whilst Norman Woolsey was third. Barry Lee raced with an experimental,

broke his National Championship jinx by taking the title at Hednesford, becoming only the second Spedeworth driver, after Barry Lee, to do this.

The third running of the Stock Saloon World Championship took place at Wisbech, in June, although it would not be third time lucky for the English Spedeworth licensed drivers. Things looked good after the draw, as grid positions placed Eddy Aldous on pole, with Belgian driver, Dirk Thomas, alongside. No one fancied a European driver to take the title, but the Antwerp-based man was a serious contender, with an engine tuned by Superstox World Champion, Antony van den Oetelaar, (Antony had retained his title at his home circuit, Tilburg, in June). It wasn't just the engine that was right either, as Dirk had spent a day converting his Escort to right hand drive specially for the event. It did the trick too, as Thomas sped away for a famous win, making it two out of three wins for the European drivers. Statistically, this probably made the Stock Saloons the most competitive short oval class across all the competing nations. Scotsman, Bob Jones, took second place from Conrad Self.

Aldous bagged the National Championship at Ipswich a month later, with Jones second again, and the other major titles were well spread out – Kevin Clarke

turbocharged Ford Pinto engine in his car and also, ever the innovator, provided some live television commentary whilst racing.

Pete Stevens remained a prolific winner in the Hot Rods, taking a third successive European title at Cowdenbeath, along with the British, English and Scottish Open Championships. Pete had, however, competed in one of the Brands Hatch PRI Hot Rod outings as a guest driver and, like Davy Evans, his thoughts were beginning to turn to competition away from the small ovals.

George Polley virtually cleaned up on the Spedeworth domestic scene, whilst Mick Collard finally

Belgian star, Dirk Thomas, won the 1984 World Stock Saloon Championship at Wisbech, and, in doing so, became the first overseas driver to beat the UK drivers to a major title on their own ground.

won the English, Jimmy Forrest the British, and Keith Jarman took the Scottish Open.

Stock Rods were beginning to gain more credibility, and, with budgets increasing at the same time, they earned their own World Championship race in 1984. The entry, however, was no more global than the first

European Championship, held at Ipswich back in 1980. It was former Superstox and Hot Rod racer, Jeff Simpson, who won that first European event, and he also took the inaugural world title at Cowdenbeath, after the car of the local hero, Ian Bell, went off-kilter. Bell redeemed himself, however, by winning the Scottish Open the

Stock Rod action at Wimbledon, and a nice variety of cars depicted. Graham Skoyles (363) heads out of frame chased by Frank Howes (Escort 44), English Champion Kevin Alexander (Fiesta 561), Jeff Simpson (Metro 303), Brian Smith (Austin 1300), and Ian Bell (Toyota).

following day. Simpson also won the 1984 British title, and was second in the season-long National Points Championship, behind Brian Smith.

There was a major shock and loss to the oval racing and rallying worlds on 21st December, when former world Hot Rod Champion, Davy Evans, and his brother Kenneth, were killed while testing a Nissan rally car for a customer, near Moira, Craigavon in Northern Ireland.

1985

The 1985 season was a fairly stable one, although there was a notable development in the formation of the International Motorsport Promoters (IMP) Group. This new body intended to standardise respective formulae, and was instrumental in introducing Superstox and Stock Rods to non-Spedeworth circuits, such as Hednesford and Buxton. Running Superstox in the North and Midlands was a great idea, but at the time, any driver from those areas wanting to race that type of car, would have been competing in BriSCA Formula Two. As a result, the Supers never became one of the domestic classes at either circuit. The Stock Rods were a different matter, however, especially at Hednesford, as the venue had plenty of drivers who waned to race Hot Rod style in an affordable class. The first race meeting for Stock Rods at 'the Hills' was on 31st March, and even included Peter Grimer, who was racing in a Metro borrowed from Spedeworth's Micky Elliott.

Down in Hampshire, Ringwood Raceway changed promoter, with former Superstox and Super Rod driver, John Coupland, co-promoting with Hot Rodder, Brian Howard. Cleethorpes Stadium, often seen as a long way north for Spedeworth and its roster of regular drivers, switched to run under the control of Vince Moody.

PRI evolved its Economy Rod class into a new formula, to be called Group A Hot Rods. Jeff Piercey won the first race in the class at Arena Essex, and went on to have a very successful season-winning both the British Championship and the Points title. The PRI 'National' Hot Rods were, of course, enjoying the long circuits at Brands Hatch and Lydden, but four of the ranks, Mick Hill, Howard Pannell, Paul Staines and Tony Paxman, also ventured to Silverstone, where the Northampton Rodders were having an early season outing as well.

The promotion also became victim of the dreaded planners, when developments at Crayford were turned down, leading to the closure of the venue. There had not even been the chance to prepare a farewell meeting, as at the last one in 1984 everyone had assumed that racing would continue the following season. The track had originally opened for Speedway and Stock Cars in 1968, with PRI taking over promotional duties two years later.

National Hot Rod driver, Pete Stevens, was really getting stuck into circuit racing, contesting the Thundersaloon Series with fellow, short circuit exponent Neil Facey, who was now registered at Northampton rather than Spedeworth, as his co-driver. The circuit formula provided mini endurance races, in saloon cars, for one or more drivers. The pair were quickly up to speed, and taking class wins, and both also continued their Hot Rod racing as well. Scottish Hot Rod ace, Graham Wait, was another to make the switch, in what was to be a long career on the circuits.

Three other, short oval characters were to make a big impression on the long circuits, in one of the most prestigious saloon car races held in the country. The Willhire 24-hour race at Snetterton was won by Superstox racer, Roy Eaton, Hot Rod and Super Rod driver, David Oates, and Northampton's racing manager, John Clark. The win was no great surprise, though, as they had finished third in the race the previous season.

The UK GP Midgets suffered a blow, when the European organisers staged a World Championship race, at Kaldenkirchen in Germany, without mentioning it to the Brits. This was a particular slap in the face to Alf Boarer, who was not only the defending champion but who, in addition to grafting as a top driver, had also been working hard as an ambassador for the formula. Dutchman, Henk Hanssen, took the crown for the third and last time in his career. Alf, nonetheless, steered his smart, BMC-powered Arrow car to a second consecutive

This picture shows Tony Paxman and Colin Watson in action at Crayford stadium, which closed its doors to racing at the end of the 1984 season.

Points title in 1985, before retiring from Midgets to move into National Hot Rods, in 2006.

It was certainly an interesting season for the Hot Rods. Ormond Christie won the World title for a third time, in an event which unusually saw the inclusion of a top American driver on the grid. Jon Leavy from Miami Beach took part in the event, and had the well-prepared Waltham Services hire car. It was clear, though, that the 1984 Limited Late Model Champion would perhaps have benefited from some build-up meetings in the UK, prior to competing with the regulars at Ipswich. Norman Woolsey took second place, with defending champion, Peter Grimer, in third. Grimer had already demonstrated his continuing class by winning the Irish Grand Prix, and he also went on to win the National at Hednesford, with Pete Stevens in second.

Former Superstox World Champion, Antony van

Three amigos win the 1985 Willhire 24-hour Saloon Car race at Snetterton. Left to right; John Clark, Roy Eaton, and David Oates.

Ulsterman, Ormond Christie, made it three wins in the Hot Rod World Championship in 1985. Here he is on the grand parade, being driven by his mechanic, Stan Woods.

den Oetelaar, made the move into Hot Rods, although without much success, and former champion Gordon Bland was tempted back into racing, competing once in the Waltham Services hire car. Bland was involved in a promotional change, when he and Aghadowey's Tommy Shaw, replaced former 'Rodder, Ernie Kilpatrick, and Robert Mathers, as co-promoters at the Ballymena Raceway in Northern Ireland. Further top names returning to Hot Rods were former West Country stars, Peter and Martin Freestone, now racing in the Midlands and equipped with state-of-the-art Toyota Starlets.

July saw the first running of the Davy Evans Memorial Trophy at Aghadowey, and the event attracted a star-studded line up. Barry Lee made his first appearance in Northern Ireland since the controversial 1979 Irish Open at the same circuit. (A large group of fans

American driver, Jon Leavy, at the Hot Rod World Championships, in the Waltham Services rental car. Jon is following Neil Facey, and being pursued by Bob Ludlam's Vauxhall Chevette.

Former Superstox Champion, Antony van den Oetelaar, switched to Hot Rods in 1985.

had been unhappy about Ormond Christie's retirement from the race, and had tried to confront him in the pits after his win.) Joining Lee on the grid, in tribute to Evans, were fellow ex-World Champions, Mick Collard and Gordon Bland, in Christie's spare car, whilst Paul Warwick made his Hot Rod racing debut in the Norman Abbot Rent-a-rod. Norman Woolsey won the main event from Pete Stevens and Keith Martin.

Warwick's Hot Rod outing

Northampton-based Hot Rodder, Phil White, was rapidly climbing through the rankings, and turned out this smart Mazda 323 for the 1985 season.

Deane Wood, working hard at the wheel of his Escort Stock Saloon at Ipswich.

Bob Jones, was the other driver who might have won! All in all, it was a good year for the Englishmen, as Ray Goudy stole the British title up at Cowdenbeath, and Titch Gardener won the European at Wisbech. Some results may have been debated, but there was never any doubting Bob Jones' ability, and he had his assured moment of glory in 1985, winning the National at Hednesford.

Unfortunately, controversy was not limited to the Stock Car World Championship. The Stock Rod event at Wisbech was 'won' by Dave Storey, who scraped into the event as a reserve, and proceeded to win by three quarters of a lap from Rindy Frost. Frost was disqualified after the event for having illegal carburettors, and subsequently banned from the sport for six months by the board of control. The legality of several of the other leading runners was called into question, and the matter

was certainly one to excite the core of the UK's short oval racing supporters, but his thoughts were, perhaps inevitably, turning towards the long circuits and a full season in single-seaters as he started to make preparations for a season in Formula Ford 1600.

At long last there was an English name on the Stock Saloon's World Championship trophy, although the race, held at Ruisbrook in Belgium, was not quite that straightforward. Alan 'Noddy' Robinson was declared the winner, but there were several different opinions as to who had actually crossed the line first – Scotsman,

was eventually examined by the sport's governing body, who declared the race result null and void. The most notable title of the season, therefore, became the National Championship, which was won by Scotland's Steve McCall, from Ian Gibbins and Brian Smith. Another Scot, Rob Gold, won the British Championship, to complete a shut out of the English drivers in the big races.

The Superstox World Championship returned to Cowdenbeath for the first time since 1980, to mark Spedeworth Scotland's 21st Anniversary. The race was rather destructive, two starts were needed after

Deane Wood always put a lot of work into his activities, and this Reliant Robin was primarily for show. Scotsman, Keith Jarman, kindly offers a lift around the circuit …

major pile-ups, and ultimately just four cars made the third start, with Vic Russell surviving to become only the second Scot to take the crown. However, as it had been held on the first of a two-day meeting, many of the visitors felt that the race should have been postponed to the following day, particularly as all four of the drivers that made it were Scots.

Robin Randall had a good season, winning his

Superstox frontrunner, Robin Randall, was one of many drivers who could be relied upon to enter into the spirit of any occasion. This Spedeweekend grand parade featured fancy dress. Randall seems to have needed some Dutch courage to assume the role of court jester.

rear wheel drive. These cars were initially only to be fitted with Pinto engines, which could also be repositioned to compensate for the heavier weight being used.

This new breed of car was intended to be far more like the road cars from which it was developed – retaining original metal body panels. The first such machine was a rear wheel drive Mk3 Ford Escort, built by renowned engineer, Sonny Howard, and the car was to be raffled with the tickets costing just £2. The draw was made at the NHRPA Championship meeting, with PRI driver, Colin Weldon, winning the prize of a lifetime.

Spedeworth's dabbling with television continued in November, when Noel Edmonds, host of the popular prime-time programme *The Late Late Breakfast Show*, featured a live stunt at Aldershot Stadium. The show staged a number of tricks over the course of the series – all involving members of the public. This particular one involved Tom Hardy, a member of the Royal Corps of Transport, stationed at Aldershot. He was strapped into a car and lifted 60-feet into the air by a crane, before being dropped down to earth, the landing being 'cushioned' by other cars.

first major titles in Superstox – the European and the National. (This was in the formula's first season of only two racing at Hednesford.) Randall was entering his most successful period in the sport, having defected from BriSCA Formula Two in the late 1970s.

The future of Hot Rod racing, and in particular the cars being used, were becoming hot topics, and a brave move to introduce a 'new breed' car was made. The *1986 Construction Rules and Regulations for Nationals* contained two big changes, aimed at significantly reducing the cost of producing a competitive National Hot Rod. Firstly, the Ford Pinto engine was uprated to give more power, making it competitive with the then-current Kent engine. In a second, and as it turned out, more successful change, front wheel drive cars could be converted to

This has to be one of the best raffle prizes of all time – Colin Weldon won the draw for a brand new Hot Rod, at the 1987 NHRPA Championship meeting.

The Spedeworth Banger brigade got a shock (or then again, perhaps not, with his credentials) when top West Country racer, Paul Shepherd, won the World Banger Championship at Wimbledon. There were, and still are, several events with the 'World' badge attached to them, but the fact that Spedeworth invited other promotions, as well as overseas drivers, always added a little more credibility to its version.

1986

A t the end of 1985, a meeting of the IMP Group paved the way for a proper Grand Prix series, including both the BriSCA Formula Two Stock Cars, and Spedeworth's Superstox. All the promoters at the meeting were happy, and a draft fixture list, with attendance and prize monies, was drawn up. The dates were tantalising; starting at the heart of Spedeworth's operation, Aldershot Stadium, next, down to Newton Abbot in Devon, and then up to Birmingham and Northampton. Two dates in Scotland would unite the fans at Newtongrange and Cowdenbeath, before another West Country round at Taunton, Buxton, Boston and Cleethorpes. Finally, there was a grand final on neutral territory at Hednesford.

Unfortunately, one party in the BriSCA promoters' camp was not happy with the proposal, and, without his support, the venture could not, and indeed did not, take place. Spedeworth did, however, go ahead and run an amended schedule under the title of the National Grand Prix Series. One BriSCA driver, Paul Phillips, defied his promotion, and got away with it, by racing at the second round, which was on shale, at Birmingham Wheels. He then went on to race the following day, under the BriSCA banner at Northampton. At the end of the season, Gerry 'Super' Cooper came out as top points scorer in the Grand Prix, with Martin Brand in second, ahead of Paul Pearson.

On a brighter note, a new circuit hit the fixtures list as Great Gidding, promoted by Northampton racing manager, John Clarke, opened its doors to formulas including the Grand Prix Midgets.

With National Hot Rod racing becoming more and more expensive, Spedeworth decided the time was right to introduce another new formula, something between the now well-established Stock Rods, and the aforementioned Nationals. The class would be

Normally seen in Stock Saloons – Keith Jarman decided to spend a while travelling in the other direction in 1986, racing Superstox.

53

SPEDEWORTH INTERNATIONAL LTD. *present the*

MOTAQUIP NATIONAL HOT ROD WORLD CHAMPIONSHIP

AND SPEDEWEEKEND 1986

SATURDAY 5 JULY AND **SUNDAY 6 JULY**

NATIONAL HOT ROD TIME TRIALS • SUPPORT EVENTS
NATIONAL HOT ROD WORLD CHAMPIONSHIP FINAL
SUPERSTOX GOLDEN AWARD AND CHAMPION OF CHAMPIONS
STOCK SALOON CARS GOLDEN HELMET
SUPER ROD BRITISH CHAMPIONSHIP
BANGER ENGLISH CHAMPIONSHIP • STOCK RODS INTERNAT'AL CUP
• **FULL RACE PROGRAMME BOTH DAYS** •

OFFICIAL SOUVENIR PROGRAMME £1

The high production values in Spedeworth's 70s and 80s Spedeweekend programmes means they have become quite collectable over the years.

powered by 1600cc engines, and appeal to drivers from Stock Rods who aspired to the Nationals, but could

not afford it. Spedeworth also saw the class appealing to former National competitors, who had retired from the sport due to the budgets now required. What was perhaps surprising was that Spedeworth did not match the new formula with PRI's Group As that had been successfully introduced the year before.

Initial impressions on the formula were not positive, although with the domestic 'National' scene suffering from reduced grids, something really had to be done, and the introduction of 1600 Hot Rods or 'Polley Rods' as they became known, was inevitable. The term came about in deference to George Polley, as it was seen as a common sense, budget formula and, as it turned out George was the first driver to win a title in the class, when he won the Southern Championship at Aldershot. The first race for the new formula, however, was in June, when Alan Dent took the chequered flag.

Budgets were an issue in Northern Ireland as well. With spectator attendances falling, the promoters decided to cut both start and prize money which, not surprisingly, went down like a lead balloon with the drivers. Most of the National Hot Rod drivers went on strike and refused to race. The two that did, Norman Woolsey and Tommy Martin, hardly had fair competition, as they shared the racetrack with the Super Rods. Woolsey himself was only racing under appeal, after his involvement in an incident at the Christmas meeting at the end of 1985.

The National Hot Rod World Championship had been a live feature of ITV's *World of Sport* programme for over a decade, but unfortunately the show was axed in September 1985, which meant no national, terrestrial coverage from 1986 onwards. Over the years, the coverage had given the sport excellent exposure, but the reality was that ITV broadcast what was only a minority sport, against the BBC's certain ratings-winner, the Wimbledon men's singles tennis final. Nonetheless,

Robert Bridger won the first semi final of the World Hot Rod Championship, at his home circuit, Lydden, in 1986. He's chased here by an unidentified Anglia, and the Escort of Paul Staines.

Anglia TV was a big fan of the racing, and it continued to cover the Spedeweekend with a regional, edited show. Spedeworth took advantage of the change in television scheduling to alter the race programme, and as a result the championship race switched to Sunday.

Before the big race, though, there was the matter of qualifying, and the 'last chance' semi finals could not have been held at two more different circuits. The first was not even held on an oval, as Lydden Circuit in Kent played host. Local track specialist, Robert Bridger, won the race from Pete Stevens and Tommy Field. The second was on the tight, Smeatharpe Raceway in Devon, and John Close, Martin Freestone and Colin Hall made it through. Norman Woolsey claimed his first World title at Ipswich in July, winning from Ormond Christie and Paul Grimer.

Jo van Rengs – winner of the 1986 European Superstox Championship, held at Tilburg raceway in Holland.

The Super Rods became the latest formula to contest a World title, and it was Pete Winstone who won at Hednesford, in April. The other two major titles in the formula went to Stu Donald, who took both the British and National titles, at Ipswich and Wimbledon respectively, after being Winstone's runner-up in the World.

Neil Bee was one of four drivers to take part in a Hot Rod test series out in South Africa. He was joined by Pete Stevens, Kevin Videan and Don Humphrey for the trip, but this was not to herald the end of his Superstox career, as he was once again top dog in that formula, winning both the World and National Championships. Robin Randall was runner-up in the World Championship, his best finish in the sport's premier race, and he won the English title on Southern soil, or rather concrete, at Arlington. The previous

season's World Champion, Vic Russell, won the Scottish Open at Cowdenbeath, whilst his countryman, Dave Moir, won the British – these were to be the last two big Superstox titles to be contested at Cowdenbeath. A suitably cosmopolitan list of major winners for 1986 was completed by Dutchman, Jo van Rengs, who won the European at Tilburg.

Spedeworth Scotland bade farewell to Cowdenbeath circuit after 22 seasons at the end of November, as the owners of Central Park declined to offer the Cecil family a new lease for the new season. The British Champion, Dave Moir, won the last Superstox race there, Malcolm Chesher just pipped George Polley to the Hot Rod final, and typically, the Stock Saloons went out with a bang – just four cars finishing a bruising race with Harry Burgoyne leading home Deane Wood.

Towards the end of the year, Wimbledon stadium hosted what was to be Spedeworth's first 'retro' evening, when competitors from past years were invited to drive modern Superstox, in an invitation race. As well as drivers, there were quite a few returning officials as well – John Clark drove the Control Car, 'Jumbo' Allen was the start marshal, and Mavis Eaton undertook lap-scoring duties. Legendary former European Champion, Tony May, won the race, and enjoyed himself so much that a comeback to racing was planned for the following season.

As ever, Wimbledon Stadium served up some superb, end-of-season racing, including the return of an old favourite idea – a 100-lap race for National Hot Rods. It had been a few seasons since Spedeworth had run the old, long distance races, with sponsorship from BP. Whilst the oil company still continued its support of a series of qualifiers, and a more traditional 'final' length race, this race was simply dubbed the Wimbledon 100. Just thirteen cars started the race, but by all accounts it

The first southwestern driver to win a major Hot Rod Championship (the 1986 English) – Ralph Sanders.

Stock Rod World Champion, Jeff Simpson, at speed in his Mk2 Escort.

was a good one, with Neil Facey taking victory. Talking of the BP Championship, there was something of a surprise this year, as Mel Cooke broke George Polley's run of four consecutive wins in the event, on 27th October at Wimbledon.

Whilst the name George Polley had been the most prominent in the list of BP winners, the 'Best in Britain' winner's list looked considerably more varied. Mick Collard (twice), Barry Lee (twice), Paul Conde and Pete Winstone had all been winners in the 1980s, and visiting drivers were also making their presence felt. Ormond Christie had taken second place in 1981, but it looked like the title would be heading back to Ulster in '86, when Keith Martin crossed the line first. This didn't happen, however, as Martin was dropped two

places in the results, due to alleged infringements, and this promoted former GP Midget Champion, Alf Boarer, to the win – a major title in his first season of Hot Rod racing. Wimbledon favourite, Salvo Falcone, took a career-best second place, with Martin third.

Ralph Sanders became the first southwestern driver to win a major National Hot Rod race, when he emerged victorious in the English Championship held on his home track, Newton Abbot. Home advantage possibly, but not in the UK Challenge Cup, which the Devonian won up in Scotland the same year.

The new 1600 Hot Rods also raced for their own version of the 'Best in Britain,' and it was one of the converts from Stock Rods, Jeff 'Slim' Simpson, who won from George Polley. Simpson, incidentally, held onto the

Some close quarter combat in the 1986 Stock Rod National Championship at Hednesford. The main focus here is the battle for second place. Eventual winner, Jim Sommerville, is already way down the road. Second is being disputed by Ian Gibbins (14), Neil Clarke (900), and Steve McCall (112).

World Stock Rod title for a third year. He didn't actually win it, as the result was declared null and void for the second year in a row, when the top four cars all failed scrutineering!

Prior to that, concerns over Spedeworth's own National Hot Rods were proved correct, as numbers dropped away at several domestic meetings. At one stage, races were held mixing the Nationals with the fledgling 1600 class, to ensure enough cars were on the grid to keep the paying public satisfied.

Spedeworth took back the World Banger crown with 'Warriors' team driver, Sean Gallagher, winning.

1986 World Champion, Sean Gallagher, looks left to see if it's safe to rejoin the fray, in a van Banger event at Wimbledon.

GP Midget action at Arena Essex. Harry Sayell (1) leads 1977 World Champion, Mick Bonner (24). Chasing them are the Sinclair brothers Peter (red) and Paul (yellow), followed by John Lowe (33) and Basil Craske (21).

Evergreen Aldershot-based racer, Roger Wilkinson, had a good season, winning both the British Figure of 8 and London Championships.

With Alf Boarer having moved to Hot Rods, it was veteran driver, Basil Craske, who took his VW-powered car to the Midgets points title he'd last held in 1983. Craske also won the World Championship at Alwalton Raceway, Peterborough – this one being organised properly, with overseas drivers being invited to take part, unlike the previous seasons!

Up country there would be a void to fill on the BriSCA circuits in 1987, as six time World Champion, Stu Smith, retired from Formula One Stock Car racing at the age of 40. His last meeting was his testimonial, at Belle Vue, Manchester, in December.

SHORT CIRCUIT

Vol. 10   October 1986   No. 7

Inside:

- **Championship round-up**
- **Steve Hunt and Eamonn Wales**
- **All the up-to-date news and views**

Short Circuit magazine has provided excellent coverage of all aspects of the sport since 1977. 1600cc Hot Rod driver, Dave Norton, will have been pleased to have made it on to the front cover in October 1986.

1987

Plans for a Superstox/Formula Two Grand Prix series were again discussed, and even made it to the BriSCA Formula Two Promoters' AGM agenda. Everyone present was in favour of the competition, but some of the key promoters did not attend, and the whole thing stalled once again. Despite this, there was plenty of cooperation between the non-BriSCA promoters; both Spedeworth and PB Promotions sent drivers along to Arena Essex to contest the oddly-named Trophyland Super Cup, where Neil Bee took the honours.

West Country promoter, Autospeed, introduced Ministox for the new season, and also renamed its Auto Rod class as Saloon Stox, to move closer in line with other promotions. Midlands promoter, Incarace, introduced a new formula called Lightning Rods, which was designed to do the job of the 1970s Economy Car class, but without contact. The formula eventually caught on in a big way, but struggled a little through the first season, with only a dozen or so regular drivers.

George Polley was honoured with a testimonial meeting, at Aldershot on 19th March, and a superb meeting, comprising National Hot Rods and Stock Saloons, saw the 'big three' of Polley, Barry Lee and Mick Collard on circuit together for the first time in years. Lee's return was courtesy of Alf Boarer, who stood aside to loan the four-time World Champion his car for the event. The meeting also included the first ever World Champion, Bob Howe, plus a couple of 1600cc Hot Rods, Micky Elliott and Jeff Simpson, who ran their cars on racing tyres.

Lee enjoyed himself so much at the Polley Testimonial that he teamed up with Boarer for a return to the sport, for a shot at the World Championship. This was a realistic proposition, as the qualifying system

Stuart Bradburn was one of the leading drivers in the Lightning Rods. This cutting from the *Wolverhampton Express and Star* celebrates his win in the Midlands Championship, at Birmingham Wheels.

had been changed: instead of a complete year of points scoring, there would be just six qualifying rounds that would take place at the start of the season. The new system was open to *all* the English drivers, rather than allowing individual promoters to send their top drivers, and meant that those who had done half a season since the last world final, would have to start again in their efforts to qualify. The positive side of the change was that the six rounds would be reminiscent of the Grand Prix Series that had been started in the late 1970s.

The early rounds were heavily subscribed, but numbers dropped away a little as some drivers realised their own chances of qualifying were becoming more remote as the events ticked away. Ricky Hunn had the honour of winning the first round at his home

Barry Lee returned to the sport in 1987, racing a Toyota Starlet for the first time. This is Barry's car, partially clothed, at the SHP Motorsport workshop.

track, Arena, and Paul Sheard won the next two, at Northampton and Buxton respectively.

The World Final itself was something of a dream result for the Spedeworth fans, as George Polley finally reclaimed the crown he had first won in 1976. The race format was changed once again, as there were two, reversed grid heats to determine the starting order for the big race. Grid positions for the heats were decided

wound up at the back of the grid for the big race.

Like many other 1980s races, controversy was not far away. Woolsey, the second-placed driver, led protests over the legality of the winner's exhaust system, and also felt that he had been baulked by some of the slower English drivers as he was lapping them. Polley's car was duly scrutineered and deemed legal, so he had the honour of carrying the gold roof for 12 months. Martin took third place, and this was regarded by many as one of the best drives of the race – he had started from 27th on the grid!

by lap trials but some of the quicker drivers came unstuck. Going for an outside line to attempt overtaking, when they could not make progress, they drifted down the order, unable to reclaim an inside line. The second heat had the slower guys at the front and, of course, they held station, which meant that the quicker drivers from the qualifying were some way back. When the points were totted up the grid seemed to alternate between fast and slow – Norman Woolsey, who had been quick in qualifying and won the first heat, started on pole, with Martin Freestone, who had been at the tail end of the qualifying times but won his heat, alongside. Two drivers who had tried to overtake in the first heat and come unstuck were Ormond Christie and Keith Martin – they

The National Hot Rod European Championship took place at Tilburg in May, and it was Sussex racer, Graham Holmes, who won the title from Ulsterman, Robin Sloan. Holmes based his racing activities on the continent, rather than at home in the UK, and also added the World Long Track title, won at Baarlo, to his list of achievements in September. Over in Northern Ireland during May, Keith Martin won the British Championship, his first major title, in the Nationals at Ballymena.

On 8th March, at the age of just 54, Former F1 and F2 driver, Trevor Frost, passed away, whilst riding a trials bike. Frost had been a star for both BriSCA and Spedeworth. He was BriSCA Points Champion in 1961, and indeed never left the top five of the chart from 1958 to 1964. He competed in six consecutive World Championships, and won the 1964 event from the back of the grid. In his Spedeworth days, he won the World International and English Championship, and was the 1966 Points Champion.

The Stock Rods had a much better season, with Jim Sommerville winning the World and National Championships, without resorting to the rulebook, whilst former Ministox racer, Mark Willis, joined the class and made an immediate impact by taking the British title, in his Mk2 Escort. Ex-Banger man, Mick Conlon, had made a very successful transition from contact to non-contact racing, and he won the English Championship held at Hednesford.

The 1600 Hot Rods were doing well, with numbers increasing and championships being introduced for the first time. Paul Osborne won the biggest title of the year – the English – at Wisbech in July, whilst Mick Conlon continued to show his class, as a non-contact driver, by winning

Two very different Stock Rods in the 1987 English Championship. Mark Willis' Escort (65) and Neil Clarke's unusual Allegro. Clarke surprised quite a few people by taking fourth on the grid after the qualifying heats.

Mick Conlon (129) was a winner in several formulae, including the 1600cc Hot Rods, where we see him battling with John Storey, Dave Longhurst (230), and Mike Rourke (140) around Ipswich.

Hertfordshire-based driver, Howard White, won the Superstox 100-lap race at Ipswich.

certainly left fans wanting more, thanks to an exciting race due to changeable weather. Martyn Brand qualified down in 15th place, and then correctly gambled on dry tyres. It was his first major win overseas, and his first big pot since winning the British in 1984. Rapid Dutchman, Ad van Besouw, was second, with Neil Bee in third.

The other Superstox titles were fairly well shared out, with Roy Eaton winning the European and National titles. Robin Randall won the British, whilst erstwhile BriSCA F2 man, Nick Lawrence, used an ex-Eaton car to win the English Championship at Ringwood, but he did not stay with the class very long. Two drivers starting to make a name for themselves, after graduating from Ministox, were John Mickel, winner of the Southern Championship, and Garry Sparkes, runner-up in the National, East Anglian and Scottish Open. The Supers also took in a 100-lap race, at Ipswich in October – this being won by Howard White, from Gerry Cooper and Neil Bee. The 'Stars of the Past' nostalgia race was won by Doug McMahon, from Alan Taylor and Fred Cracknell.

Bob Jones became the first driver in Stock Saloons to retain the World Championship. He'd won the first one on home ground, at Cowdenbeath, but won the 1987 title at Buxton, and the run of testimonial meetings for long-serving drivers continued, with one for Horry Barnes, who had been racing for over thirty years.

the East Anglian Championship. Spedeworth and PRI arranged a couple of meetings in which their respective 1600cc and Group A Hot Rods raced together, and any differences in engine specification were seemingly cancelled out by tyre performance. At 1250cc the Group As were giving away 350cc, but they had racing tyres, as opposed to the 1600cc Hot Rods' road rubber.

Venue closures were not limited to the UK as, after 16 seasons of racing, Germany's Kaldenkirchen circuit became victim to environmental pressure at the end of the season. The World Superstox Championship held in September was the last meeting there, and

One of the Spedeworth Spedeweek programmes which spectators could use as a guide to an entire week's worth of racing. The promotion adopted this weekly format back in 1972. The principal meeting in week 43, 1987, was the Stock Car English Championship, and Superstox 'Stars From The Past' race.

The Spedeworth Formula One Stock Cars had had a great year, thanks in some measure to the increased credibility gained by sharing key fixtures with Hot Stox. This was, after all, how major championships used to be decided – invite other promotions and tracks to race together occasionally. The key event for the formula was the British Championship at Wimbledon in October, when former BriSCA World Champion, Len Wolfenden, (Hot Stox) took the title from Peter Scott (Formula One). The top six places were shared equally between the visiting and host formulae. Scott won quite a few races, including the East Anglian, Southern and Western Championships, whilst Marty Page won the English.

Bob Jones won the Stock Saloon World Championship for the second year in succession, in 1987. He's not having things so good here at Cowdenbeath, a couple of seasons later.

65

1988

After three seasons co-promoting at Ringwood Raceway, John Coupland found himself out of a job, as Brian Howard teamed up with the circuit's owner, Reg Slack, to run racing at the Hampshire venue. Supporters at Birmingham Wheels were looking forward to watching racing on a new asphalt surface, Super Rods joined the Hot Rods in having 'National' as a prefix to their title, and PRI announced a series of dates, at the Swindon Speedway track, which would include Superstox, Group A Hot Rods and Bangers.

Cornish fans had to face the new racing season without visits to St Austell, which had closed to make way for a retail development. The Cornish Stadium had been one of the sport's first venues, and had hosted the Formula Two World Championship twice in the 1970s. There were, however, hopes of a new F2 track in the

Barry Lee's odd-looking Toyota Starlet, dubbed the 'speedboat,' had tongues wagging when it first appeared in the 1988 qualifying series.

Fast becoming one of the superstars of Hot Rod racing in 1988, Northampton-registered Phil White in the pit area at Arena, Essex.

county, as Trevillett Raceway, near Tintagel, applied for IMP Group membership – the 390-yard shale circuit was based in a disused quarry.

Before the regular season got under way, there was another test series against the South Africans, although this time it was an all-Ulster team that travelled – Ormond and Adrian Christie, Keith Martin and Robin Sloan. The lads took a convincing 6-1 win in the series.

Irish star, Leslie Dallas, returned to National Hot Rod racing after a brief foray into Rallycross, following a ban from the short ovals, and the Collard name was back in the winner's circle. This time, though, it was Rob, son

of 1980 World Champion Mick, who was picking up race wins down at Matchams Park, in his Mk2 Escort.

The Hot Rods again contested a six-round qualifying campaign for the World Championship, and these were followed by two semi finals, at Arena and Hednesford. There were still questions over the format which, in theory, allowed drivers who had done very little in the way of racing throughout the season, to make it through to the big race. The flip side of this was that entries did not tail off substantially, as the qualifying rounds progressed.

Phil White was the man on a mission at the World Championship weekend; he was second fastest in the lap

Surrey driver, Carl Pratt, broke ranks from the hordes of Toyota Starlets and Escorts, by racing this neat Ford Fiesta.

As the decade came to a close, there were fewer Talbot Sunbeams in action. This one was raced by 1987 Winternational winner, Frank West.

Arena Essex-based driver, Ricky Hunn, was, at this stage, another emerging star of the national Hot Rods, having worked his way up over the years through the ranks of the Anglia and Group A Hot Rods.

The ever popular Jeff Simpson – a driver who won championships, Stock Rods, 1600cc Hot Rods and national Hot Rods. This picture is from 1998 – the year he won the Hot Rods Winternational.

trials and won the first heat, which, coupled with a decent finish in the second, earned him pole position for the big race on the Sunday. The weather conditions were dreadful – not what you would expect for early July – but White was ready for whatever an English summer could throw at him, and he duly drove off to victory. Drive of the race was from George Polley, who showed all his race craft to come through, from a lowly grid position, to take second.

Just a week prior to winning the Hot Rod title, White had accepted an invitation to race a brand new Sierra, in the Super Rod World Championship. The race was billed as 'open', and with nowhere near as many registered drivers as the Hot Rods, all you had to do was turn up to race – no qualification necessary. No less than six drivers in the event were contesting their first Super Rod race of the season that day. Regular or not, White duly beat all the regulars, taking the title at his first attempt.

The other Hot Rod titles found a variety of homes, with Jeff Simpson winning the Winternational to get his season off to a good start. Phil White added the National, in its silver jubilee year, to his brace of World titles, and Phil Morgan won the British

Another driver who would take the top level of short oval racing by storm in the 1990s – Kent-based brick haulier, John Steward.

1984 World Champion, Peter Grimer, about to embark on some practice at Arena.

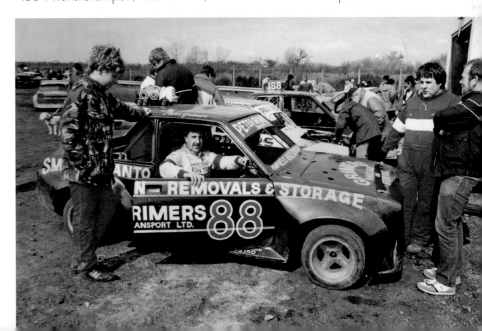

For many Hot Rod fans, the attraction was the action. This photo captures what you rarely see on the MSA-controlled circuits, groups of cars racing close together, with both inside and outside lines being used.

Championship, putting home knowledge to good use at Newton Abbot. Neil Facey won both the English and NHRPA titles, whilst the Ulster drivers were virtually shut out of the majors, although Ormond Christie did take the European crown at Ballymena in May.

Superstox racing was well and truly dominated by Martyn Brand, who the won World, European, National, British and English Championships. It has to be said that the European scene, in particular, was at its weakest for several seasons – only two continental drivers raced with

14 visitors from the UK in the European championship at Tilburg, in May that year. Only the minor silverware found a home away from the Brand household, Alan Cayzer won the Winternational at Wimbledon early in the year, whilst Rob Perry won the Southern Championship at Arlington.

Another 100-lap race was also held for the class at Ipswich, with Neil Bee taking the honours. Unusually, Brand's World title win is largely overlooked, as most people remember the race, held at Arlington, for other reasons. Garry Sparkes had qualified on pole, with Dutchman, Ad van Besouw, alongside. The big talking point, however, was the growing feud between Roy Eaton and Rob Perry. The pair had barely completed a lap of the big race before finding themselves in the fence, for the second time in a fortnight – Eaton's car was virtually two thirds of the way through. The drama did not stop with the Perry/Eaton incident though, as van Besouw was disqualified from second place for using polished con-rods.

From con-rods to Conrad ... More controversy at the Stock Saloon World Championship, as Conrad Self won the race, but was disqualified for using Bilstein front struts on the 636 car. Deane Wood, who had been a close second, inherited the title.

Yarmouth became host to a World final for the first time in nine years, when the Stock Rods contested their gold roof event at the seaside venue. Melly Cooke ran out winner, and also passed scrutineering, although the second-placed car, that of Mick Copsey, did not.

There were more promotional changes in Scotland, as Kenny Stewart took over at the helm of Spedeworth's Armadale circuit. Nigel Cecil had kept his upcoming retirement a closely guarded secret, and only announced his departure at his final meeting on 4th September, bringing 24 years of promoting by the Cecil family to an end.

Short Circuit magazine cover from July 1988. Conrad Self was first across the line in the Stock Saloon World final, though subsequently disqualified.

1989

On 1st January 1989, a major rule change came into being for the National Hot Rods, the minimum length of cars was reduced to 11ft 6in. This was intended to encourage drivers to use body styles of cars that were still in production, and, together with the allowance of front to rear wheel drive conversions, permitted the use of the Peugeot 205 and the latest Ford Fiesta.

Scottish fans were without Newtongrange Stadium as the 1989 season started. The local authority took the decision not to grant planning permission again in January, and it looked like all was lost for the GMP promotion, although there was a glimmer of hope, as Knockhill circuit were looking at the possibility of running Stock Cars. Just a month later GMP were back in action, not at Knockhill, but at Central Park, Cowdenbeath, the former home of Spedeworth Scotland. To ensure it happened, Gordon McDougall had taken over the football club and bought the pit area, which had been earmarked for housing. The raceway duly reopened, with the legendary 'Racewall', to a near-capacity crowd.

In Northern Ireland, for the second time in a decade, the season opened with the whole sport mourning the loss of a star driver. Leslie Dallas was shot dead at his garage business in Coagh, County Tyrone, on 7th March. He was 38 years of age, and had been racing in Hot Rods for just over a decade.

Simon Johnson had been racing the first Peugeot 205 'National' in 1988 under an experimental licence, and he continued racing with it as the new rules came into force. The Grimer brothers were amongst the first to take advantage of these, and debuted smart Ford Fiestas built by Sonny Howard and sponsored by Belvoir Autocar, who had shown a keen interest in 'new breed' style Hot Rods a couple of seasons back, albeit on the independent Alwalton Raceway. Another of the more unusual cars to debut was the Empress Racing prepared Toyota Starlet of Nigel Smith. The car looked unusual, as

One of several UK circuits lost to drivers and spectators in the 1980s, Newtongrange, or 'Nitten,' as it was known. Stock Saloon drivers, George Chirray and Graham McCabe, head the star-graded drivers under the yellow flags.

The first Peugeot 205 Hot Rod was raced by Spedeworth's Simon Johnson.

The luxury of two cars for Paul Grimer, at the Arena World Championship qualifier. Nearest the camera is the Ford Fiesta, which was brand new and still under development at the time. Paul's tried and trusted Toyota Starlet is behind.

Nigel Smith's controversial 'holey' Empress-built Toyota Starlet.

The Peugeot 205 quickly became established as a popular model to have in Hot Rods – it looked good and went well. Here is Mick Collard's fine example.

it had hundreds of holes in the panels to lighten it, but it was the construction that was attracting attention, as both front and rear chassis sections were built from tube, rather than being original.

Mick Collard was back, out and about on the racetrack, although he was now registered with Northampton Stadium rather than Spedeworth, as he could only commit to weekend racing. The Hot Rods again contested regular rounds to qualify for the World Championship, followed by two, higher points scoring semis. The rounds were very well attended, with 65 cars engaging for the opening qualifier at Arena Essex, where George Polley won both his heats and the final. Not surprisingly, there was a lower turn-out at Newton Abbot for round two, but even the tiny racecourse circuit attracted 51 entrants, which perhaps showed that National Hot Rod racing was at something of a peak, and in great shape to move into the 1990s.

Colin White won that round, and the following one at Birmingham, whilst Phil White took the Hednesford event. Polley took round five at Ipswich, whilst Neil Facey won the last one at Northampton. Colin White was the top points scorer from these half-dozen events, but a further two double-points rounds would determine the final qualifiers – at Newton Abbot and Wisbech. Numbers were slightly down at the first, but 41 cars at Newton Abbot was not really a problem – especially for Ricky Hunn, who won the final. Following the second semi, it was Polley who emerged as the top English points scorer.

The World title, however, was heading over to Northern Ireland again, as Hot Rod racing's 'Grandad', Norman Woolsey, won the title, and it was a first class delivery for his new sponsor. Woolsey's Royal Mail-liveried cars are probably the most recognisable brand to have been carried on the short ovals. Facey took a

Sadly, the Mk3 Ford Escort never made it as a top line Hot Rod, despite the efforts of drivers such as Mick Cannon who produced a well turned-out version. Mick leads Mark Peck, Bryan Wright, Ken Salter, and Mike Beeston in this shot.

Who needs a jack, when you've got loads of spare rims and tyres? The car of Jason Dell, 1987 Best in Britain winner, is ready for some under-car diagnostics.

The Royal Mail-liveried Peugeot 205 of 1989 World Champion, Norman Woolsey.

career-best second in the world, and Colin White, giving notice of what was to come in future years, took third.

Barry Lee made another return to Hot Rod racing, in a one-off appearance at the inaugural 1600cc Hot Rods World Championship, at Ipswich. The title went to Alan Dent, who also won the British Championship, also at Ipswich, later that year.

Ray Goudy became an English hero by winning the Stock Car World Championship up at Armadale, whilst Harry Burgoyne returned the compliment by taking the National at Hednesford. Conrad Self's 12-month ban from racing, after his disqualification from the 1988 World Final, was quashed, but he did not return. The Stock Cars 1989 controversy arose in the European

His first world title is nearly ten years away at this point, but Colin White was the top points scorer in the first stage of qualifying for 1989's big race.

Tony Allard leads Andrew Dance, Andy Harris, Nigel Murphy, Steve Dance and Danny Brosnan in one of the Hot Rod World qualifiers.

Championship at Birmingham Wheels, when Willie Barnes was initially awarded the win but, after the race video and lap charts were revisited, Steve O'Dell actually took the title.

The Super Rod World Championship attracted an American entry, as Californian Jamie Pfeifer, having a three week stay in the UK, took to the grid in a Rover. Sadly, the car was not the most competitive, and it was

Californian Stock Car racer, Jamie Pfeifer, became the first US representative in the Super Rods World Final, when he took part in the big race at Hednesford Raceway, in summer 1989. Despite the unfamiliarity of clockwise racing and a borrowed Rover V8 car – regarded as uncompetitive against the lighter V6 Sierras and Capris – he was running well, before mechanical trouble ended his race.

business as usual for the regulars. Phil White was back, defending his title, and it was he and Tim Foxlow who won the heats. White took pole position for the big race, and it looked like he might repeat the win, but he got carried along by a back marker moving from the outside line to the infield, and this allowed former Irish Banger Champion, Wilson Hamilton, through to take the lead. White rejoined not too far back in second, but

Garry Sparkes swept all before him in 1989 to win all the major championships, although this shot was taken a little earlier in his career.

any chance expired with his engine, which seized, as he crossed the line as runner-up.

Back in the National Hot Rods, Phil White's year was by no means a lean one, as he won both the British and English titles to keep his name at the forefront of the sport. Colin White won the Best in Britain, whilst

Neil Facey took the National. It had been a good season for Hot Rod racing, and the future looked bright, with drivers registering with one body and with **solus** dates throughout the season.

That was until a split in the ranks occurred, on 30th November. The Northampton promotion was unhappy

A crowded home straight, full of Superstox at Ipswich. Spedeworth's original formula is showing that nearly thirty years' worth of development had done no harm at all. Alan Canham leads the pack.

at plans for doing away with domestic racing, stating they wanted to "Run Hot Rod racing all year round, not just on a handful of dates controlled by someone else." Northampton's cars were also running at Lydden Circuit, and a stand-alone series was announced, with cars effectively running to Hot Rod rules, but with windscreens. The class was to be known as Intersaloons, and several drivers pledged their allegiance to the new formula.

'Sparkes Flies' was the ubiquitous headline for the Supers, as Garry Sparkes steered car 612 to all the major titles with the exception of the English Championship, which was won by Martin Brand. This was just the start of an incredible career in the formula for the young man from Bury St Edmunds, although he was to be regularly challenged throughout the 1990s, so the open-wheelers were far from becoming a one horse race.

The decade came to a sad end in December 1989, when Spedeworth's Ted Weaver lost his battle with cancer. Ted had been one of the real characters of the sport, starting as a spectator but soon becoming involved in the organisation, and he worked his way through several roles; Scrutineer, Steward, Auto Spedeway team Manager, Start Marshal and Director.

Although not everybody wanted to cooperate and work together, the 1980s will be seen as the decade when most promoters realised it was better to run classes to similar rules. Travelling up and down the country certainly became easier, that helped the regular exchange of drivers and gave a great deal of credibility to the many championships that were being staged. Although there were more formulae for drivers to choose from to race in, conversely there were fewer venues to visit. In England alone, the 1980s saw the closure of White City (Manchester), Crewe, Blackburn, Crayford, Leicester, Rochdale, Cleethorpes, Belle Vue (Hyde Road), St Austell and Aycliffe.

Racing had completely changed since the early seventies. Gone were the cheap and cheerful vehicles that meant that top drivers could actually make a living from racing. Cars were now technically sophisticated and professional looking, but as the crowds had dropped away over the years, there was less gate money for the

Spedeworth International proudly present the
1989 BANGER CHAMPIONSHIP OF THE WORLD
AT WIMBLEDON STADIUM
Sunday 5 November 1989 - 7.00pm

The Captain, Terry Coke, defending Banger World Champion.

Souvenir Programme
50p

One of the last big race meetings of the decade was the Spedeworth version of the World Banger Championship, on 5th November at Wimbledon. Tim Coates was the winner.

promoters to put back into the sport, as start and prize money. Nonetheless, the sport was as colourful as ever, and ready to move into the 1990s.

Appendix – The Champions

Formula	Championship	Year	Circuit	Winner
Hot Rods	World	1980	Ipswich	Mick Collard
		1981	Ipswich	Ormond Christie
		1982	Ipswich	Davy Evans
		1983	Ipswich	Ormond Christie
		1984	Ipswich	Peter Grimer
		1985	Ipswich	Ormond Christie
		1986	Ipswich	Norman Woolsey
		1987	Ipswich	George Polley
		1988	Ipswich	Phil White
		1989	Ipswich	Norman Woolsey
Hot Rods	European	1980	Northampton	Mick Collard
		1981	Newton Abbot	Ormond Christie
		1982	Ballymena	Pete Stevens
		1983	Belgium	Pete Stevens
		1984	Cowdenbeath	Pete Stevens
		1985	Kaldenkirchen	Graham Holmes
		1986	Buxton	Leslie Dallas
		1987	Tilburg	Graham Holmes
		1988	Ballymena	Ormond Christie
		1989	Tilburg	Anthony v d Oetelaar
Hot Rods	National	1980	Hednesford	Trevor Shaw
		1981	Hednesford	Pete Stevens
		1982	Hednesford	Pete Stevens
		1983	Hednesford	Pete Stevens
		1984	Hednesford	Mick Collard
		1985	Hednesford	Peter Grimer
		1986	Hednesford	Norman Woolsey
		1987	Hednesford	George Polley

Formula	Championship	Year	Circuit	Winner
		1988	Hednesford	Phil White
		1989	Hednesford	Neil Facey
Hot Rods	NHRPA Series	1980	Various	Barry Lee
Hot Rods	NHRPA Championship	1981	Ipswich	Colin Facey
		1982	Ipswich	Peter Grimer
		1983	Ipswich	Leslie Dallas
		1984	Ipswich	George Polley
		1985	Ipswich	Leslie Dallas
		1986	Ipswich	George Polley
		1987	Ipswich	George Polley
		1988	Ipswich	Neil Facey
		1989	Ipswich	Norman Woolsey
Hot Rods	British	1980	Hednesford	Trevor Shaw
		1981	Arena	Barry Lee
		1982	Buxton	Davy Evans
		1983	Newton Abbot	Mick Collard
		1984	Ballymena	Pete Stevens
		1985	Northampton	Norman Woolsey
		1986	Cowdenbeath	Norman Woolsey
		1987	Ballymena	Keith Martin
		1988	Newton Abbot	Phil Morgan
		1989	Cowdenbeath	Phil White
Hot Rods	English	1980	Buxton	Barry Lee
		1981	Wisbech	Stu Jackson
		1982	Northampton	Pete Stevens
		1983	Wisbech	Peter Grimer
		1984	Hednesford	Pete Stevens
		1985	Arena	George Polley
		1986	Newton Abbot	Ralph Sanders
		1987	Northampton	Phil White
		1988	Northampton	Neil Facey
		1989	Wimbledon	Phil White
Superstox	World	1980	Cowdenbeath	Dave Pierce
		1981	Kaldenkirchen	Neil Bee
		1982	Cleethorpes	Neil Bee
		1983	Cleethorpes	Antony v d Oetelaar

Formula	Championship	Year	Circuit	Winner
		1984	Tilburg	Antony v d Oetelaar
		1985	Cowdenbeath	Vic Russell
		1986	Wisbech	Neil Bee
		1987	Kaldenkirchen	Martyn Brand
		1988	Arlington	Martyn Brand
		1989	Wisbech	Garry Sparkes
Superstox	European	1980	Ploegsteert	Dave Pierce
		1981	Ballymena	Dave Pierce
		1982	Cowdenbeath	Dave Pierce
		1983	–	Dave Pierce
		1984	Cowdenbeath	Les Clark
		1985	Tilburg	Robin Randall
		1986	Tilburg	Jo van Rengs
		1987	Arlington	Roy Eaton
		1988	Tilburg	Martyn Brand
		1989	Tilburg	Garry Sparkes
Superstox	British	1980	Ipswich	Jim Welch
		1981	Wimbledon	Bill Bridges
		1982	Wimbledon	Dave Willis
		1983	Cowdenbeath	Neil Bee
		1984	Cleethorpes	Martyn Brand
		1985	Wisbech	Paul Warwick
		1986	Cowdenbeath	Dave Moir
		1987	Armadale	Robin Randall
		1988	Armadale	Martyn Brand
		1989	Wimbledon	Garry Sparkes
Superstox	National	1980	Ipswich	Derek Hales
		1981	Ipswich	Brian Randall
		1982	Not held	–
		1983	Ipswich	Tony Roots
		1984	Ipswich	Paul Warwick
		1985	Hednesford	Robin Randall
		1986	Hednesford	Neil Bee
		1987	Wisbech	Roy Eaton
		1988	Wisbech	Martyn Brand
		1989	Armadale	Garry Sparkes

Formula	Championship	Year	Circuit	Winner
Superstox	English	1980	Wimbledon	Howard White
		1981	Wisbech	Brian Randall
		1982	Wimbledon	Dave Turner
		1983	Wimbledon	Jim Davey
		1984	Wimbledon	Bert Hawkins
		1985	Wisbech	John Gray
		1986	Arlington	Robin Randall
		1987	Ringwood	Nick Lawrence
		1988	Arena	Martyn Brand
		1989	Arena	Martyn Brand
Stock Cars	World	1982	Kaldenkirchen	Detlev Katstein
		1983	Cowdenbeath	Gordon Brown
		1984	Wisbech	Dirk Thomas
		1985	Ruisbrook	Noddy Robinson
		1986	Cowdenbeath	Bob Jones
		1987	Buxton	Bob Jones
		1988	Wisbech	Deane Wood
		1989	Armadale	Ray Goudy
Stock Cars	European	1980	Not held	–
		1981	Not held	–
		1982	Not held	–
		1983	Kaldenkirchen	Bert Houben
		1984	Kaldenkirchen	Dirk Jacobs
		1985	Wisbech	Titch Gardner
		1986	Kaldenkirchen	Loui Haggen
		1987	Wisbech	Keith Jackson
		1988	Armadale	Ernie Burgoyne
		1989	Birmingham	Steve O'Dell
Stock Cars	National	1980	Not held	–
		1981	Not held	–
		1982	Ipswich	Robert George
		1983	Ipswich	Conrad Self
		1984	Ipswich	Eddy Aldous
		1985	Hednesford	Bob Jones
		1986	Hednesford	Ernie Burgoyne
		1987	Hednesford	Kevin Clarke

Formula	Championship	Year	Circuit	Winner
		1988	Hednesford	John Howarth
		1989	Hednesford	Harry Burgoyne
Stock Cars	British	1980	Cowdenbeath	Keith Jarman
		1981	Ipswich	Graham Overy
		1982	Cowdenbeath	John Burns
		1983	Cleethorpes	Keith Jarman
		1984	Cowdenbeath	Jimmy Forrest
		1985	Cowdenbeath	Ray Goudy
		1986	Wisbech	Tony Jones
		1987	Armadale	Conrad Self
		1989	Wisbech	Geoff Morris
Stock Cars	English	1980	Wimbledon	Joe Fuller
		1981	Wimbledon	Dick Doddington
		1982	Ipswich	Eddie George
		1983	Not held	–
		1984	Ipswich	Kevin Clarke
		1985	Not held	–
		1986	Buxton	Mick Brassey
		1987	Aldershot	Kevin Shinn
		1988	Arena	Steve O'Dell
		1989	Boston	Ray Goudy
Bangers	World	1980	Wimbledon	Darwin Melbourne
		1981	Wimbledon	Nick Linfield
		1982	Wimbledon	Chris Colliver
		1983	Wimbledon	Graham Lashley
		1984	Wimbledon	Sean Liddiard
		1985	Wimbledon	Paul Shepherd
		1986	Wimbledon	Sean Gallagher
		1987	Wimbledon	Roger Wilkinson
		1988	Wimbledon	Terry Coke
		1989	Wimbledon	Tim Coates
Stock Rods	World	1984	Cowdenbeath	Jeff Simpson
		1985	Wisbech	David Storey (null)
		1986	Arlington	Ron Harris Jr (null)
		1987	Armadale	Jim Sommerville
		1988	Yarmouth	Mel Cooke

Formula	Championship	Year	Circuit	Winner
		1989	Tilburg	Norman Hicks
Stock Rods	European	1980	Ipswich	Jeff Simpson
		1981	Not held	–
		1982	Not held	–
		1983	Cleethorpes	Ian Bell
		1984	Germany	Ad van Besouw
		1985	Not held	–
		1986	Not held	–
		1987	Not held	–
		1988	Armadale	Ian Bell
		1989	Hednesford	Dave Longhurst
Stock Rods	National	1980	Not held	–
		1981	Not held	–
		1982	Ipswich	Don Larby
		1983	Cleethorpes	Brian Smith
		1984	Not held	–
		1985	Hednesford	Steve McCall
		1986	Hednesford	Jim Sommerville
		1987	Hednesford	Jim Sommerville
		1988	Hednesford	Mick Conlan
		1989	Hednesford	Brian Smith
Stock Rods	British	1980	Wimbledon	Brian Smith
		1981	Cowdenbeath	David Storey
		1982	Cleethorpes	Ian Bell
		1983	Armadale	Ian Bell
		1984	Wimbledon	Jeff Simpson
		1985	Cowdenbeath	Robert Gold
		1986	Ringwood	Ron Harris Junior
		1987	Ringwood	Mark Willis
		1988	Birmingham	Ian Bell
		1989	Boston	Graham White
Stock Rods	English	1980	Aldershot	Dave Bayliss
		1981	Ipswich	Jeff Simpson
		1982	Not held	–
		1983	Not held	–
		1984	Ipswich	Kevin Alexander

Formula	Championship	Year	Circuit	Winner
		1985	Wisbech	Mel Cooke
		1986	Wisbech	Kevin Alexander
		1987	Hednesford	Mick Conlon
		1988	Not held	–
		1989	Wisbech	Keith Rolfe
1600 Hot Rods	World	1989	Ipswich	Alan Dent
1600 Hot Rods	British	1988	Ipswich	Dave Storey
		1989	Ipswich	Alan Dent
1600 Hot Rods	English	1987	Wisbech	Paul Osborne
		1988	Yarmouth	Dave Longhurst
		1989	Wimbledon	Graham White
Formula One	British	1980	Yarmouth	Les Mitchell
		1981	Wimbledon	Alan England
		1982	Not held	–
		1983	Cleethorpes	Stu Blyth
		1984	Not held	–
		1985	Wisbech	Brian Bennett
		1986	Wimbledon	Peter Scott
		1987	Wimbledon	Len Wolfenden
		1988	Ipswich	Alan England
Formula One	British	1989	Ipswich	Terry O'Connor
Ministox	World	1988	Wisbech	Tony Theed
		1989	Wisbech	Peter Dodge
Ministox	European	1984	Birmingham	Diggy Smith
		1986	Wisbech	Mark Thorpe
		1987	Arlington	Roy Fuller
		1988	Not held	–
		1989	Armadale	Gordon Gay
Ministox	National	1985	Hednesford	Steve Carding
		1986	Hednesford	George Boult
		1987	Hednesford	Jon-Paul Cooper
		1988	Birmingham	Carl Overy
		1989	–	Gordon Gay
Ministox	British	1982	Yarmouth	Alan Mickel
		1983	Wimbledon	Paul Warwick
		1984	Arlington	Mike Armstrong

Formula	Championship	Year	Circuit	Winner
		1985	Cowdenbeath	David Brown
		1986	Buxton	Carl Overy
		1987	Wisbech	Roy Fuller
		1988	Armadale	Carl Overy
		1989	Newton Abbott	Mark Bouldon
Super Rods	World	1986	Hednesford	Pete Winstone
		1987	Hednesford	Bill Smith
		1988	Hednesford	Phil White
		1989	Hednesford	Wilson Hamilton
Super Rods	European	1980	Kaldenkirchen	George Polley
		1981	Ipswich	Gordon Bland
		1982	Cleethorpes	Pete Winstone
		1983	Not held	–
		1984	Not held	–
		1985	Not held	–
		1986	Ringwood	Stu Donald
		1987	Buxton	Wilson Hamilton
		1988	Not held	–
		1989	Not held	–
Super Rods	National	1980	Wimbledon	George Polley
		1981	Hednesford	Tim Foxlow
		1982	Hednesford	Larry Dewsbury
		1983	Hednesford	Tim Foxlow
		1984	Hednesford	Pete Winstone
		1985	Hednesford	Stu Donald
		1986	Hednesford	Stu Donald
		1987	Hednesford	Wilson Hamilton
		1988	Hednesford	Wilson Hamilton
		1989	Hednesford	Stu Donald
Super Rods	British	1980	Ipswich	Paul Conde
		1981	Wimbledon	Dick Hillard
		1982	Ipswich	Pete Winstone
		1983	Northampton	Jon Brookes
		1984	Not held	–
		1985	Buxton	Dave Dimmick
		1986	Ipswich	Stu Donald

Formula	Championship	Year	Circuit	Winner
		1987	Ipswich	Hoss Parry
		1988	Skegness	Stu Donald
		1989	Skegness	Stu Donald
GP Midgets	World	1980	Northampton	Basil Craske
		1981	Recklinghausen	Henk Hanssen
		1982	Swaffham	Mick Bonner
		1983	Kaldenkirchen	Wilfred Hofer
		1984	Northampton	Alf Boarer
		1985	Kaldenkirchen	Henk Hanssen
		1986	Peterborough	Basil Craske
		1987	Kaldenkirchen	Jan Schraets
		1988	Peterborough	Klaus Kilianski
		1989	Posterholt	Basil Craske

More *Those were the days ...* titles from Veloce Publishing –

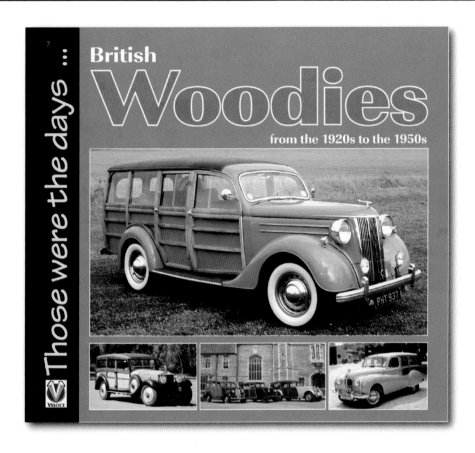

Highlighting the work of hundreds of small coachbuilders, and illustrated with 100 rare and previously unpublished photos, this book is a tribute to the skills of the people who built these amazing wooden wonders.

£12.99
ISBN: 978-1-845840-38-9

For more info on Veloce titles, visit our website at www.veloce.co.uk
email info@veloce.co.uk • tel: +44 (0)1305 260068 • prices subject to change • p+p extra

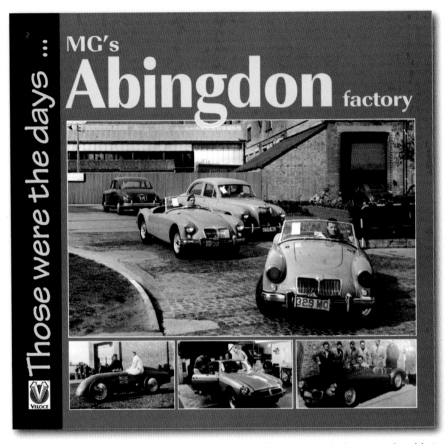

The MG, from being a Morris car modified in the corner of a backstreet workshop, evolved into a sports car in its own right. The 160 pictures in this book – many never seen before – chronicle every aspect of the MG Abingdon factory, from its opening amidst great euphoria in 1930 to its closure amidst great recrimination in 1980.

£12.99
ISBN: 978-1-845841-14-0

For more info on Veloce titles, visit our website at www.veloce.co.uk
email info@veloce.co.uk • tel: +44 (0)1305 260068 • prices subject to change • p+p extra

Those were the days ...

Motor Racing at
Oulton Park
in the 1960s

Oulton Park was one of the last circuits to play host to non-championship Formula 1 races. Set in beautiful Cheshire parkland, it was a favourite with the celebrated drivers of the era and with spectators who could watch their heroes compete on a true road cicuit.

£12.99
ISBN: 978-1-845840-38-9

For more info on Veloce titles, visit our website at www.veloce.co.uk
email info@veloce.co.uk • tel: +44 (0)1305 260068 • prices subject to change • p+p extra

More *Those were the days ...* titles from Veloce Publishing –

Those were the days ...

Motor Racing at
Oulton Park
in the 1970s

Featuring over 150 colour and black & white photographs, many previously unpublished, the book recalls this period of consolidation at the beautiful Cheshire circuit.

£12.99
ISBN: 978-1-845840-38-9

For more info on Veloce titles, visit our website at www.veloce.co.uk
email info@veloce.co.uk • tel: +44 (0)1305 260068 • prices subject to change • p+p extra

INDEX